This book is dedicated to Geoffrey Lewth

THE GREAT NORT
RAILWAY IN THE
WEST RIDING

Martin Bairstow

N1 0-6-2T No 69474 pilots B1, 4-6-0 No 61280 through Queensbury with a nine coach excursion from Halifax to Morecambe on 21 May 1955, the last day of normal passenger service.   *(Peter Sunderland)*

Published by Martin Bairstow, 53 Kirklees Drive, Farsley, Leeds
Printed by Amadeus Press Ltd, Huddersfield, West Yorkshire

Introduction

The Great Northern Railway was incorporated in 1846 to provide a more direct route from London to Leeds and York than that which had been available since 1840 via Rugby and Derby.

By 1852, the Company had completed what we now know as the southern section of the East Coast Main Line between Kings Cross and Doncaster. Great Northern trains were obliged to continue their journeys to Leeds and York by running powers over rival lines because the company's own plans to reach these cities direct had, for the time being, been frustrated.

Once it had established its foothold in the West Riding, the Great Northern went on to build a local network much of which was heavily engineered, scenic, steeply graded, and a test for the locomotives and crews who had to work it.

Unfortunately, many of the West Riding towns reached by the Great Northern were also served by other railways which had arrived earlier, often by easier and therefore faster lower lying routes.

The Great Northern Railway disappeared as an independent company at the end of 1922 though the name tended to live on to describe that part of the LNER and British Railways. Even today, post privatisation, suburban services out of Kings Cross are operated by the West Anglia Great Northern Railway. Although the main line and London suburban routes thrive, little remains of the West Riding network. The only former Great Northern route still functioning is between Doncaster, Wakefield, Leeds and Bradford. Other towns continue to be rail served: Halifax, Keighley, Shipley, Morley, Batley, Dewsbury, Castleford. But in every case it was the Great Northern line which succumbed to rationalisation in the 1950s and '60s leaving the tracks of its one time rival companies to carry today's much enhanced frequency of passenger trains.

None of the closed Great Northern branches have been preserved nor converted into footpaths or cycle ways. A few buildings survive in new uses such as Thackley and Shipley stations, Low Moor and Keighley goods sheds. Many of the more imposing earthworks still stand including the viaducts at Thornton, Hewenden, Cullingworth and Tingley. It is still possible to see some of the bricked up tunnel mouths. If, whilst exploring these remains, you are in need of a drink there are pubs at Stanningley, Thackley, Ingrow and Thornton still called 'The Great Northern' as a reminder of their proximity to long abandoned stations.

This book aims to recreate some of the atmosphere of the Great Northern West Riding network whilst bringing up to date the story of the surviving stretch of line between Doncaster, Leeds and Bradford.

I am grateful to everybody who has helped with the book. The photographs and other contributions are credited individually. Glynis Boocock again typed the manuscript from my scribble.

Farsley, Leeds

Martin Bairstow
October 1999

N1 0-6-2T No 69434, crossing Hewenden Viaduct with the 4.18pm Keighley to Bradford Exchange on 14 May 1955. *(J.C.W. Halliday)*

Trainee Clerk
John Holroyd finds his first employment at Dewsbury Central

The search is on for my first job and British Railways have sent me a free rail ticket from Leeds to York and return. A bus ride from home in Gildersome takes me to City Station and the 09.15 'North Briton' arriving York 09.46. There are about twenty of us hopefully assembled at the Railway Institute for a brief introduction and an aptitude test in the main hall at 10.30. Happily this proved no great hardship and I left at 12.40 for a bite of lunch, a visit to the nearby Railway Museum properties and drifted home to await results.

A week later, Friday 16 September 1955, another free ticket takes me on the 12.42 train from Leeds to the York Railway Offices. Here I face an interview panel and medical examination and again head for home in anticipation. On Monday 19th a letter arrives saying I have been accepted as a Trainee Clerk and this is followed on Wednesday by a letter from Leeds Aire Street offices. I immediately don my coat and go to Leeds where I have another short interview and learn that my training will commence at Dewsbury Central Station on Monday 26 September. It just remained for me to collect an insurance card from Morley Youth Employment Office and cycle to Dewsbury to locate the Central Station for my first day at work.

The relief Station Master made me welcome at 09.00 on Monday and showed me round. His office was in the main platform buildings whereas my base was to be the Booking Office at ground level with only the overhead rumble of trains and the cries of the market traders for entertainment.

There was plenty of work to be done by the clerical staff, parcels traffic occupying a lot of our time, principally fibre boxes for the local dyers and cleaners' factories. Market traders parked their equipment trolleys under the arches for a weekly rental and Coal Waybilling for Hickleton Colliery was a daily chore.

I learned how to 'Take Off' a balance against ticket, parcel label and luggage-in-advance transactions. The first ticket I sold was a single to Lincoln at 9s. 11d. Fares were printed on the regular stock of tickets but less usual destinations had to be looked up in the fares manual and then uplifted to the present-day charge by reference to the current conversion booklet. If there was not a fare listed for any destination it was necessary to send a 'Faro' telegram to head office to request the base value which was then written in the manual.

The ticket racks had to be kept topped up from the main supply in drawers beneath the window. Consecutive numbering needed checking with each new batch and orders placed for more tickets as stocks dwindled. All our tickets were Edmundson cards which needed dating at the moment of sale – on both ends in the case of returns. Ordinary singles and returns were green, Day tickets blue, Excursions cream and Zones (Dog, Bicycle or Pram tickets) were red.

Monday evenings I attended 'Passenger Station Work and Accounts' classes at the Leeds Aire Street Offices between 18.30 and 19.30. Tuesday evenings likewise was 'Goods Station Work and Accounts.' I had a free pass for the train to Leeds valid on these days.

First week's pay amounted to £3 5s. 2d. Lunch at the nearby Playhouse Restaurant cost 3s. 1d. inclusive of coffee at this time.

There were four clerks involved in running the Office. Fred Ingham (to Cleckheaton) was replaced by Bill Donelly (from Headingley) as Chief Clerk on 17 October. The other three clerks, alternating early, middle and late turns, were Tom Howells of

The staircase leading up to the island platform at Dewsbury Central. *(John Holroyd)*

Thornhill, Bill Boden of Westerton and Jack Waterworth from Morley. I took on middle turn, 10.00-18.30, from Monday 19 December. Early turn ran from 6.30 to 13.00 (6.30 to 12.15 Saturdays). Late turn was 15.30-22.00 (Starting 14.00 Wednesdays). Porters were on duty earlier and later than the clerical staff so I never needed a key.

On Monday 28 November 1955 Station Master E.N. Pearson took over from the reliefs and he took me under his wing until I was transferred to Stanley in January 1956. Eric went on to Bridlington a couple of years later and stayed there until his retirement.

Occasional errands to check parcel deliveries with our associates at Wellington Road; The collecting of 6d. outstanding account from Newton Studios; Much laughter from Eric, the Undertakers' Suppliers lad; Upheaval during repainting; Two days when the Auditors dropped in . . . All served to relieve our otherwise daily routine. My cycle rides from Gildersome to start early turn on icy mornings were a good lesson in steering without wobbling. My last day at Dewsbury Central was Saturday 28 January 1956 when I did the coal waybills and filled in the weekly 'Pink Return.' This form compared the current weeks' figures with those of the same week last year, expecting an explanation of any major fluctuations.

I was instructed to report to Stanley Station on Monday 30 January as assistant to the regular clerk at this busy time in the Rhubarb Season. My father and I cycled to locate Stanley on the Sunday in readiness for my move. The round trip, with a variety of permutations, was about 18½ miles.

I arrived at the deserted station at 09.00 and porter 'Young' Bill emerged from the Lamp Room to welcome me and took me to the Station Master's House door. Albert Tate was in the middle of shaving but invited me in and his wife provided a mug of tea. I then had a conducted tour of the site which comprised a signal box working the level crossing at the east end of the platforms, a goods shed, sidings on both up and down sides and the smallest booking office imaginable! At least there was a good view of passing trains!

Methley South Station came under the care of Stanley's S.M. There was a signal box here and two lady porters dealt with all passenger and parcel traffic. Two or three times a week the Stanley clerk used a free pass to ride along to Methley to balance the books and this job was shown to me on my first afternoon. Regular clerk Brian Padgett and I boarded the push and pull train (Loco 69696) and dealt with Methley's finances returning on the same (Castleford-Leeds) train at 14.49.

As my attendance at Passenger and Goods evening classes continued I developed a routine of travelling to Stanley by public transport on Mondays and Tuesdays, cycling on the other days I worked. Usually I would walk to Morley Top for the 07.51 or 09.52 train to Wakefield (B1-hauled), continuing to Stanley by B&S bus (fare 4½d.). I only once took advantage of my cycle permit for the train from Morley Top. In the evening the 17.31 train took me to Leeds, my ticket being an original Methley Joint Privilege Single costing 5d. I travelled home from the Leeds evening class by Yorkshire Woollen District bus which picked up in Aire Street.

Soldiers on parade at Ardsley Station.   *(Martin Bairstow Collection)*

'Black Five' No 45140 calls at Morley Top with the up 'White Rose' (Bradford Exchange to Kings Cross) on 31 December 1960, the day the station closed. *(D. Holmes)*

In February the printed stock of Leeds Day Returns ran out and we had to hand write blank day returns until more arrived. Although Beeston station was closed by this date we still sold tickets to Holbeck for passengers alighting at Beeston when Leeds United had a home football match.

My pay for the first week of February was £3 15s. 2d. inclusive of an increase of two weeks. I assisted the S.M. in making out staff payslips and obtaining insurance stamps from nearby Lake Lock Post Office. In addition to the staff at Stanley and Methley South (Clerks, Porters, Night Shunter, Signalmen) we also paid the level crossing keeper at Patrick Green on the E&WYU line half a mile to the north.

We booked in boxes of rhubarb from about 15.30 to 18.30 when the engine came to collect our vans and take them to Ardsley. 'Old' Bill got his pipe going and we had a roaring fire in the goods office stove. About a dozen local growers would fill three or four vans most nights and usually one on Saturday mornings. Occasionally we would be given a few sticks to take home. I twice relieved at Ardsley during this period and was required to telephone the full list of assembled rhubarb van numbers to Leeds Control. At about 20.45 the vans from various local stations had been marshalled for Kings Cross and Covent Garden. A clerk plodding up the sidings with a hand-held paraffin lamp would be frowned upon nowadays!

Although there were some commuters who would have travelled earlier in the day, I never sold a passenger ticket at Ardsley on my middle turn. But I did receive an enquiry from a young lad who came to the window asking if I knew the number of the A3 which had just gone by.

Brian Padgett handed in his notice so I held the fort until clerk Laurie Palmer started on 26 March. That afternoon I took him on the push and pull to learn the Methley bookkeeping procedure. 4-4-2T

67438 was working the train. Station Master Tate had the Ladies Waiting Room converted into an office for his personal use, a new outer door giving access to the Ladies toilets. He 'threw away' the Ladies Waiting Room sign and I still have it as a tangible reminder of those days.

Wednesday 28 March was the morning of my exam in Goods Station Work and Accounts at Leeds College of Commerce. The Passenger Accounts exam was on Thursday 5 April. On Easter Monday 2 April I sold 71 tickets for the 12.06 Half-Day Excursion to Scarborough. Just 16 passengers booked for a similar train on Tuesday. The Methley ladies didn't sell any tickets on either day but still claimed their overtime to see the trains back in the evening!

My visits to Ardsley allowed me to copy out a list of all the month-end forms which had to be compiled and, with the assistance of S.M. Stebbings of Lofthouse we established an acceptable routine. A copy of this list served me well over the coming year when I moved to Morley Low as a fully fledged clerk.

Stanley station closed on 31 October 1964. Albert Tate had moved to Arbroath and we kept in touch for many years until both he and then his wife, Polly, died. The station house remained in a ruinous condition until finally demolished to make way for new housing: 'The Chase', Aberford Road.

Dewsbury Central's market facade remains to this day. The main arches with their iron gates, the booking office window and smaller washroom window are infilled with stone. The main A638 Inner Ring Road runs along the course of the track and platforms.

An account of John's days at Morley Low Station can be found in the second edition of 'The Leeds Huddersfield & Manchester Railway – The Standedge Line' published in 1990 in the same series.

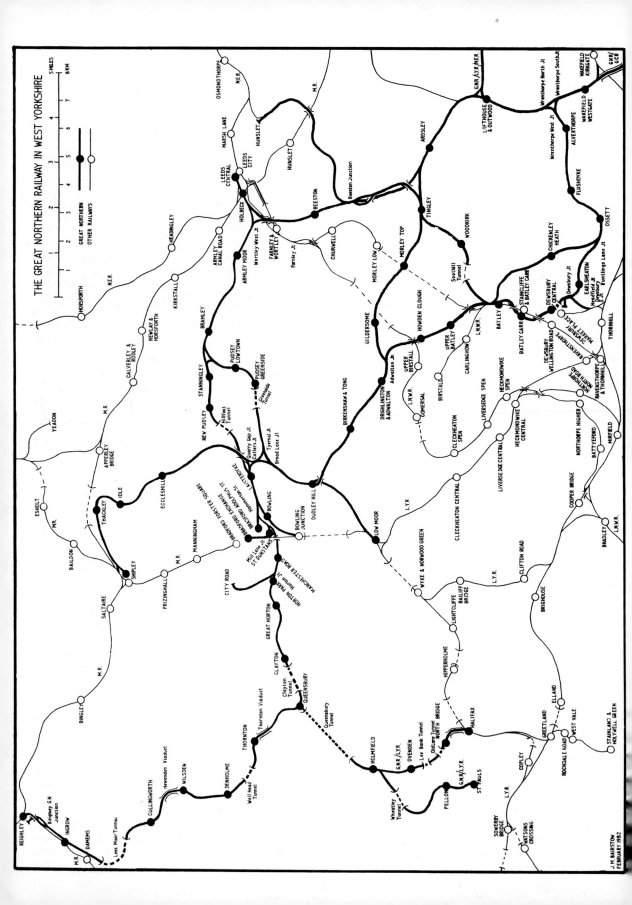

THE GREAT NORTHERN RAILWAY IN WEST YORKSHIRE

GREAT NORTHERN
OTHER RAILWAYS

J.M. BAIRSTOW
FEBRUARY 1982

Leeds Central

A4 No 60029 'Woodcock' prepares to leave Leeds Central with the 'White Rose' for Kings Cross on 16 March 1963.

(Martin Bairstow Collection)

For most of its 119 year existence, Central Station served primarily as the Great Northern terminus in Leeds. It catered also for the Lancashire & Yorkshire and Great Central Railways both of whose trains came into Leeds by running powers over the GNR.

Leeds Central was owned and had been built by four companies, two of whom abandoned it before it was even completed.

The first station in the centre of Leeds was at Wellington, opened by the Midland Railway on 30 June 1846. At that time, four other railways were in the course of promotion or actual construction. All four were heading towards Leeds where they desired to build a joint Central Station at a prestige site fronting onto Park Row.

The four companies were:

(1) The Great Northern Railway.

(2) The Leeds, Dewsbury & Manchester Railway, part of the Standedge Route, which was authorised in June 1845, incorporated into the London & North Western Railway in July 1847 and opened on 18 September 1848.

(3) The Manchester & Leeds Railway, which in 1847 changed its name to the Lancashire & Yorkshire Railway, had obtained powers in August 1846 for a line into Leeds from Bowling Junction, near Bradford. This line was eventually opened on 1 August 1854. It was used by the Lancashire & Yorkshire Railway but came into the ownership of the Great Northern.

(4) The Leeds & Thirsk Railway, which became part of the North Eastern in 1854. This was authorised in 1845 and completed on 9 July 1849.

These four embryonic companies deposited a Parliamentary Bill in November 1846 for their joint station on the north side of Wellington Street. The Leeds Central Station Act was passed on 22 July 1848 permitting the purchase of a significant area of land around what is today York Place, Park Place, King Street and Infirmary Street.

When the Dewsbury line opened on 18 September 1848. plans for the Central Station had not progressed at all so temporary facilities had to be provided on the south side of Wellington Street. These became the terminus both for the London & North Western Railway from Huddersfield and for the Lancashire & Yorkshire Railway whose trains from Manchester via the Calder Valley took advantage of this new route into Leeds via Mirfield and Dewsbury.

The same temporary station was also used by the Leeds & Thirsk Railway from 9 July 1849. Arriving trains used the Gelderd Curve to climb up from the Midland.

Last of the quartet of companies to run into the temporary Leeds Central Station was the Great Northern whose trains approached over the Midland Railway from Methley Junction, taking the south side of the triangle to avoid Leeds Wellington (the present goods line avoiding Leeds Station) then proceeded towards Armley before reversing direction and running up the Gelderd Curve to gain access to Central Station. This operation began on 1 October 1849, four weeks later than planned because of the 'Methley Incident.'

By the first half of 1850, with still no progress on the permanent Central Station, there were four companies using the temporary one. The Leeds & Thirsk was the first to express dissatisfaction by moving its business to the Midland Railway's Wellington Station from 1 May 1850. This simply involved their incoming trains staying on the Midland into Wellington instead of turning up the Gelderd Curve.

Five months later, the London & North Western Railway was able to effect a similar change with the opening of the curve between Copley and Whitehall Junctions. They also used Wellington from 1 October 1850.

The North Eastern (successor to the Leeds & Thirsk) and London & North Western continued to use Wellington until the opening of their own joint station at Leeds New on 1 April 1869.

Despite their pulling out of Leeds Central Station the North Eastern and London & North Western Railways remained joint owners of it. They both retained goods depots at or near to Leeds Central, the London & North Western on the high level adjacent to the passenger station on the north side, the North Eastern (originally Leeds & Thirsk) a little further north at a lower level with access from the Gelderd Curve.

The Great Northern also built a goods depot, between the Leeds & Thirsk and London & North Western establishments. It too was dissatisfied with passenger facilities at the incomplete Central Station. So on 14 May 1850 it withdrew from the joint ownership and transferred its passenger trains to its own temporary station built alongside its goods depot on the low level.

This meant that from 1 October 1850 the only company actually using the high level Central Station was the Lancashire & Yorkshire with its trains from Manchester arriving via Dewsbury.

Plans were dropped for the prestige Central Station, north of Wellington Street fronting on to Park Row. Instead a permanent structure was built on the site of the temporary one and completed by June 1852.

The Lancashire & Yorkshire Railway had hoped to build its own line direct to Leeds Central from Bowling Junction, near Bradford. It was unable to raise finance to achieve this. Instead the route was built by the independent Leeds, Bradford & Halifax Junction Railway. When this opened on 1 August 1854, it was worked by the Great Northern Railway. Like many small railway companies, the Leeds, Bradford & Halifax Junction preferred to remain as owners but not operators.

The new line approached Leeds alongside the London & North Western, crossing over the Midland at Holbeck then actually joining the LNWR at the entrance to the high level Leeds Central Station. Access to the low level GNR passenger station would have involved setting back down the Gelderd Curve then going forward again – an impractical proposition. So the GNR made peace with the three old Central Station partners, resumed its role as a quarter share owner and transferred all passenger traffic back to the high level station from 1 August 1854.

The Lancashire & Yorkshire Railway also remained at Central Station but from 1854 it approached by a different route. Trains from Manchester Victoria came via Halifax and Bowling Junction rather than via Dewsbury.

A1 4-6-2 No 60117 'Bois Roussel' pulling away from Leeds Central with 'The Queen of Scots Pullman'.
(Peter Sunderland)

The End of Leeds Central

Up until the mid 1950s, it had been considered impractical to concentrate all traffic on one station in Leeds. However, *Trains Illustrated* (May 1957) confirmed that British Railways were at last about to embark upon such a scheme. The August 1959 issue gave details of the plan which had been approved.

Central Station was to close and business was to be concentrated on Leeds City where passengers and parcels would be segregated. Passengers would use an enlarged facility at what was then known as City South – the former LNWR/NER New Station. City North, the old Wellington would be given over to handling parcels.

In order to get trains from the former Great Northern routes, from Doncaster and Bradford Exchange into Leeds City, a flyover was planned from near Holbeck High Level, crossing over the Midland thereby segregating passenger trains from the heavy flows of freight from the north via Skipton towards Normanton. A completion date of 1963/4 was hoped for.

Some work was carried out including the new canal bridge at the entrance to Leeds City reducing the number of tracks at this critical point from six to four. Also, an additional through platform was built on the outside of the train shed at City South. Then, in 1961, work was suspended.

Modern Railways (September 1963) announced a fresh go-ahead with a 1965 completion date. The scope of the work had been reduced chiefly by eliminating the flyover, forcing Great Northern traffic to descend a new Whitehall curve alongside Holbeck High Level. Trains from Doncaster were

afforded a different route into Leeds by commandeering the former LNWR line over Farnley Viaduct and connecting it to the GN at the new Gelderd Road Junction. This was eventually found not to help and was abandoned with electrification.

The new arrangements finally came into effect on Monday 1 May 1967. Leeds Central had closed early on the evening of Saturday 29 April and there had been only limited services into and out of Leeds City on the Sunday.

The 'New' Leeds City

Ever since 1967, the facilities at the 'new' Leeds Station have been criticised both for poor passenger amenities and inadequate capacity to handle the volume of trains.

The subway steps are a serious impediment to anyone who is elderly or encumbered with luggage or small children. In theory you can ask for assistance but in practice can easily miss your train in the process.

The station and track layout were designed at a time when rail travel was in the doldrums, when most local trains were expected to be withdrawn. Since 1967, most services have doubled or trebled in frequency. The only way they keep going at all is that they have better acceleration and can clear the critical junctions more rapidly.

Since the mid-1980s, there has been a plan to increase the number of platforms and to create six tracks instead of four at the western approach. Finally, in 1999, Railtrack have embarked upon this major change which will also see better station facilities including much needed passenger operated lifts.

The last passenger train from Leeds Central, the 6.10pm dmu for Harrogate explodes detonators as it departs on Saturday 29 April 1967.   *(John Holroyd)*

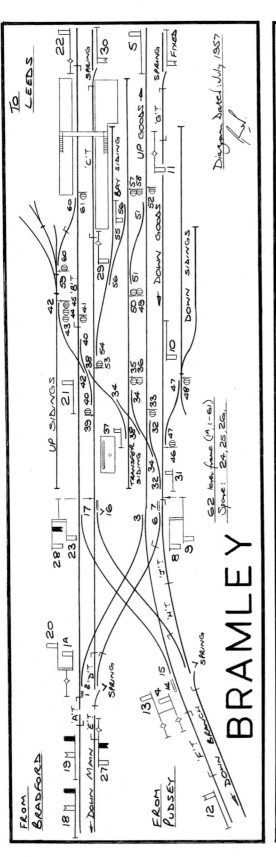

BRAMLEY

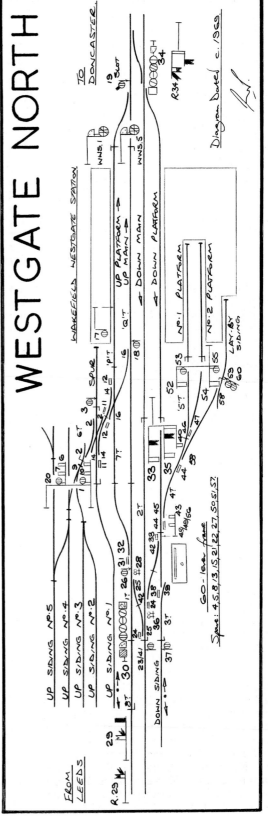

WESTGATE NORTH

The Leeds, Bradford & Halifax Junction Railway

B1 4-6-0 No 61129 passing Armley Moor with the 1.20pm (Sundays) Harrogate to Kings Cross, diverted via Bowling Junction because of engineering work on 31 December 1961. *(D. Holmes)*

This was the project which enabled the Great Northern Railway to begin consolidating its foothold in the West Riding.

By an Act of 1846, the Manchester & Leeds Railway (soon to be renamed the Lancashire & Yorkshire) had been authorised to build a line from Sowerby Bridge through Low Moor, Laisterdyke and Stanningley to Leeds. There was to be a branch from Bowling into Bradford. In the event the route from Sowerby Bridge to Bradford was completed by 1 January 1852 but no progress was possible on the link between Bowling Junction and Leeds. The Lancashire & Yorkshire sought powers to abandon this and other West Riding projects for which it could not raise finance.

The failure of the L&Y to reach Leeds disappointed supporters who had assisted the company in gaining authorisation for the Bowling Junction to Leeds line. In November 1851 they deposited their own Bill for the nominally independent Leeds, Bradford & Halifax Junction Railway which effectively took over the L&Y powers between Bowling Junction and the entrance to Leeds Central. The project had the support of the Great Northern Railway which seized the opportunity to gain direct access into Bradford, thus projecting itself into territory which previously had looked as though it would fall to the L&Y.

The Leeds, Bradford & Halifax Junction Railway Act was passed on 30 June 1852. Running powers were granted over the London & North Western Railway from Holbeck into Leeds Central and over the L&Y from Bowling Junction to Halifax. In return, the L&Y was afforded running powers from Bowling Junction to Leeds Central.

A second Act of 4 August 1853 authorised a branch from Laisterdyke to Bradford Adolphus Street and confirmed arrangements by which the Leeds, Bradford & Halifax Junction would be worked by the Great Northern Railway.

The line opened to the public including the Bradford branch, on 1 August 1854. Ten trains per day (four on Sundays) were operated each way between Leeds Central and Bradford Adolphus Street. In addition, the Lancashire & Yorkshire Railway diverted its main line traffic from Manchester via the Calder Valley away from the Dewsbury route, which it had been using since 1848, running instead through Halifax, Bowling Junction and over the LB&HJ.

The route is heavily graded with a climb of 1 in 50 from Holbeck to Armley followed by 3½ miles at 1 in 100 to the summit at Laisterdyke. From there the 'main line' to Bowling Junction fell, initially at 1 in 100, whilst the branch into Bradford Adolphus Street fell at 1 in 44. The biggest engineering work,

N1 0-6-2T No 69483 at Leeds Central on 7 September 1953.   *(G.M. Staddon/N.E. Stead Collection)*

79504/79004 on the 3.35pm Bradford Exchange to Leeds Central at Bramley on 14 June 1954, the first day of regular diesel operation.
(D. Holmes)

Armley Moor looking towards Bramley. From the 1890s until 1968 there were four tracks between Wortley West and Bramley. The goods lines, on the left, did not have platforms at Armley Moor nor Bramley.
(Geoffrey Lewthwaite)

Fairburn 2-6-4T No 42107, of Low Moor Shed, powers up the 1 in 100 through Bramley en route for Liverpool Exchange via Bowling Junction and the Calder Valley route 1957.　*(A.M. Ross)*

Stanningley for Farsley, looking towards Bradford. The mill, once rail served, stands on what is now the ASDA Supermarket!
(Geoffrey Lewthwaite)

13

is the 450 yard Stanningley Tunnel sometimes called Hillfoot.

An insight into early operating procedure, or lack of them, is given in a report by the directors into a collision at Bradford Adolphus Street during the formal opening celebrations on 31 July 1854. An engine got out of control on the 1 in 44 gradient from Laisterdyke and damaged passenger coaches in the terminus.

The driver had not been over the line before and was totally unacquainted with the gradients. The whole proceeding is characterised by a general want of knowledge of the line and especially of the gradients, which in some parts require care and skilful management. Your committee are of the opinion that somewhat more caution might have been used by all concerned in the management of the Railway on the day of opening.

Despite opposition from the Lancashire & Yorkshire Railway, the Leeds, Bradford & Halifax Junction was absorbed into the Great Northern by an Act of 5 July 1865.

Adolphus Street was convenient neither for Bradford City Centre nor for the interchange with other railways. In 1864, the LB&HJ had obtained powers for the ³/₄ mile link between Hammerton Street and Mill Lane Junction whence running powers were obtained over the L&Y into Exchange Station. This opened on 7 January 1867. From that date Adolphus Street was used only for goods although it seems from our later examination of the Shipley Ledger that it may have been used for overflow passenger traffic because of extreme congestion at Exchange Station.

This problem was finally resolved in 1888 when the new ten platform station was completed at Bradford Exchange. The approach from Mill Lane Junction was widened to accommodate separate pairs of tracks for the L&Y and GN Railways. Preparation for this involved the opening out of the 133 yard tunnel in 1884.

In 1910, there were typically two trains per hour between Leeds Central and Bradford Exchange but there was no regular pattern whatsoever. Some trains stopped only at Stanningley, some ran all stations via Pudsey but this was not a hard and fast rule. There were also some stopping trains via Stanningley. There were quite a number of trains covering only part of the route with some starting and terminating at Bramley or Stanningley.

'Black Five' 4-6-0 No 44693 is ready to leave Bradford Exchange in 1967 with 'The Yorkshire Pullman' which it will take as far as Leeds.
(D.J. Mitchell)

13 Lancashire & Yorkshire trains left Leeds Central via Stanningley and Bowling Junction. These varied in status from locals going no further than Sowerby Bridge to the 'Vestibule Luncheon Car Train' which left at 1.00pm for Liverpool Exchange. The 'Belfast Boat Train' departed at 8.05pm for Fleetwood. This, too, conveyed a restaurant car and, after calling at Holbeck, ran first stop Halifax which was reached in 28 minutes, faster than any of today's trains.

There was, by 1910, only one Great Northern train between Leeds Central and Halifax via Bowling Junction. It was the decline in the local GN service which had led to the closure of Bowling Station in 1895. L&Y expresses did not stop there.

If we go forward to June 1953, the timetable pattern is similar but with slightly fewer through trains and none of the short workings. Some of the intermediate stations had long intervals between trains. There was no local service at all on Sundays – just two through trains from Kings Cross to Bradford and five trains from Leeds Central on the former Lancashire & Yorkshire service but with no intermediate stops between Leeds and Low Moor.

This was the standard of service at a time when bus services were at their zenith and car ownership had recovered from the effects of wartime petrol shortages.

Change was at hand. From 14 June 1954, the route between Bradford Exchange, Leeds Central and Harrogate was the scene of the first full scale deployment of diesel multiple units on British Railways. The eight 'Derby Lightweight' twin car sets 79000-7 and 79500-7 were described in *Railways Around Harrogate Volume Three*. They offered a half hourly frequency between Bradford Exchange and Leeds Central going forward to Harrogate hourly. They also gave a stopping service between Bradford and Leeds via Pudsey almost at hourly intervals. They ran on Sundays – through to Knaresborough in Summer – but with no intermediate stops between Bradford and Leeds.

Steam trains continued from Leeds Central to Manchester and Liverpool until they, in turn, were replaced by class 110 diesel multiple units from 1 January 1962. Operating hourly from Harrogate, these trains were incorporated into the existing diesel service. They travelled via Bradford Exchange leaving only one early morning mail/passenger train using the direct Laisterdyke to Bowling Junction route. This finally closed to passenger traffic in 1969 and to goods in 1985 having latterly been reduced to a single line with no actual junction at Laisterdyke.

Stanier 2-6-4T No 42616 heads the 10.23 Bradford Exchange to Kings Cross through St. Dunstans in 1967. The Queensbury line curves in from the left. *(D.J. Mitchell)*

A three car 'Calder Valley' dmu passing Quarry Gap in March 1962. It has just gone under the Shipley branch and is approaching Laisterdyke. *(Peter Sunderland)*

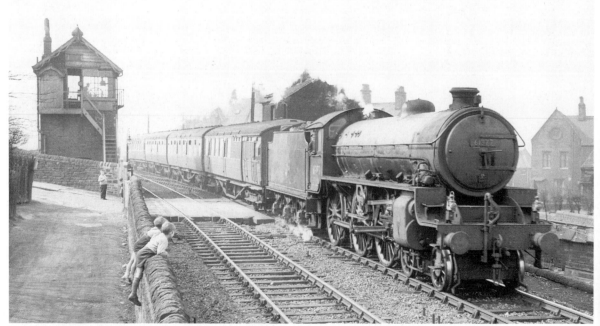

B1 4-6-0 No 61377 passing Hall Lane, between Bowling Junction and Laisterdyke with a Doncaster to Leeds Central local on 5 April 1959. It was diverted via Thornhill and Low Moor due to Bridge work at Wortley South. *(Peter Sunderland)*

Laisterdyke Station looking towards Bradford in 1870.
(Frank Kipling Collection)

The cutting had to be widened for the new station opened in 1892. Paget Foulds, Station Master, is nearest the camera.
(Frank Kipling Collection)

A class J3 0-6-0 climbing to Laisterdyke in July 1945 with a local, probably for Leeds. The route from Bowling Junction is on the left   *(R Hardy)*

Doncaster, Wakefield and Leeds

Class A3 4-6-2, No 60114 'W P Allen' recovering from a temporary speed restriction south of Sandal with the 'White Rose' from Leeds Central to Kings Cross in 1957.
(A.M. Ross)

The Great Northern Railway first reached Leeds Central from Doncaster on 1 October 1849 by running powers over the Lancashire & Yorkshire and Midland Railways via Askern and Methley Junction. The present day route via Wakefield Westgate came about later in two separate stages.

The Bradford, Wakefield & Leeds Railway

The title is confusing as this railway never served Bradford. It did, however, have its offices in Bradford. It was closely associated with the Leeds, Bradford & Halifax Junction Railway with which it connected by a triangular junction at Wortley, about a mile out of Leeds Central. It ran through Ardsley to Wakefield Westgate before curving to join the Lancashire & Yorkshire Railway at Ings Road Junction, just west of Wakefield Kirkgate.

The line opened on Saturday 3 October 1857. It was worked by the Great Northern Railway who, from 1 November, diverted their London trains this way to avoid both dependence on the Midland Railway and the reversal at Gelderd Junction outside Leeds Central. Great Northern traffic from Doncaster now travelled over the L&Y via Askern, Knottingley, Featherstone, Wakefield Kirkgate and Westgate.

The Bradford, Wakefield & Leeds Railway was responsible for building the line from Wakefield to Batley. It also promoted the Methley Joint (see later chapter). In 1863 it changed its name to the West Yorkshire Railway.

In common with the Leeds, Bradford & Halifax Junction, the West Yorkshire enjoyed mixed relations with the Great Northern. On occasions both small companies threatened to break off the working arrangements with the GN and operate their own lines. To a partial extent they did but then had to hire rolling stock from the GN. For its part, the Great Northern threatened the West Yorkshire that it would go back to running via Methley Junction if condition of the track did not improve between Wakefield and Leeds.

Such problems were brought to an end in 1865 when the Great Northern took over the two small companies. They cannot have been all bad as they had both installed block signalling on all their lines prior to being absorbed.

The West Riding & Grimsby Joint

The Great Northern had failed in 1857, 1860 and 1861 to gain Parliamentary sanction for a direct Doncaster to Wakefield line.

On 7 August 1862, such powers were granted to the nominally independent West Riding & Grimsby Railway. The 'main line' was to run from Wakefield Westgate to Stainforth & Hatfield (between Doncaster and Scunthorpe) and so provide access

Doncaster Station comprises two large island platforms connected by a subway to the main buildings which are on the east side (to the right in this photo). Class A3 4-6-2 No 60059 'Tracery' stands in platform 4 with an express for London Kings Cross about 1961. *(J.C.W. Halliday)*

Photographed from the platform end at Holbeck High Level on 18 July 1953, A3 4-6-2 No 60062 'Minoru' has just left Leeds Central with an express for London Kings Cross. *(F.W. Smith)*

from the West Riding to Grimsby. A 'branch' was to run from Adwick Junction to Doncaster. The scheme had financial backing from the South Yorkshire and the Manchester, Sheffield & Lincolnshire Railways.

The Great Northern attempted to purchase the West Riding & Grimsby whilst under construction but would probably have been frustrated in Parliament by opposition from the Manchester, Sheffield & Lincolnshire which was in the process of taking over the South Yorkshire Railway. The solution was for the GN and MS&L jointly to purchase the West Riding & Grimsby which they did with effect from 1 February 1866, the day that the Wakefield to Doncaster section opened. Immediately the Great Northern diverted its London to Leeds traffic via the new line thus finally achieving its ambition of a direct route of 185¾ miles between the two cities, entirely under its own control. The Adwick Junction to Stainforth link opened in November 1866 permitting the MS&L to run a through service between Grimsby and Leeds. Part of the agreement for the joint line had included MS&L running powers from Wakefield Westgate into Leeds Central.

No 63633 joins the West Riding & Grimsby at Hare Park Junction in 1955 with a train off the link from Crofton Junction. *(A.M. Ross)*

Class A3 4-6-2 No 60077 'The White Knight' passing Ardsley Engine Shed and South Box with an express from Kings Cross to Leeds in July 1961. *(Peter Sunderland)*

The signalman and train recorder ('booking lad') inside Wakefield Westgate South Box, 1959.

(A.M. Ross)

Viewed from the box, J39 No 63612 approaches with a coal train from Barnsley via Nostell.

(A.M. Ross)

The West Riding & Grimsby Joint building survived at South Elmsall until the early 1980s but then the station became unstaffed and the building was demolished.
(Martin Bairstow)

The original Sandal station, closed in 1957.
(Martin Bairstow Collection)

Driver Bob Foster and fireman Wilf Webster, both of Copley Hill Shed, wait to restart the 11.20 Doncaster to Leeds Central at Wakefield Westgate in 1944.

(R. Hardy)

2-2-2 No 879 stands in Wakefield Westgate at the head of an express from Leeds Central to Kings Cross. Built at Doncaster in 1894, the Stirling 'Singles' were designed for express work on lightly graded lines.
(Martin Bairstow Collection)

60029 'Woodcock' passing the closed (but still occasionally used) station at Beeston with a Leeds Central to Doncaster local on 17 June 1961.
(Martin Bairstow Collection)

C14 4-4-2T No 67438 passing Beeston Junction with a local from Leeds Central.
The junction signal is for the Batley branch. The line curving to the right behind the train is the Hunslet goods branch opened by the Great Northern on 3 July 1899.
(A.M. Ross)

Between Bradford and Wakefield

Under a lowering sky, 45338 and 42084 climb away from Dewsbury towards Wakefield with the 8.52 (SO) Bradford to Cleethorpes on 11 August 1962.   *(M. Mitchell)*

A reasonably direct route via Wortley was available between Wakefield and Bradford from the opening of the BW&L on 3 October 1857. Just one week later, a shorter but even steeper route was completed via Morley. Over the next 23 years, the Great Northern completed two more variants of the Wakefield to Bradford route, first via Ossett and Batley then via Dewsbury. The Lancashire & Yorkshire Railway also opened a direct Wakefield to Bradford route in 1869 when it completed the short link between Thornhill and Heckmondwike.

In more recent times all five of the routes just mentioned have been abandoned. Wakefield and Bradford are still connected by a rail but only via Leeds albeit that trains on both segments of the journey now run at an unprecedented frequency.

It was the coalfield and heavy industry that drew the railway into the area between Wakefield and Bradford. A branch from Laisterdyke to Gildersome was authorised by the Leeds, Bradford & Halifax Junction Act of 4 August 1853. Double track from its opening on 19 August 1856, the five mile line was steeply graded with short tunnels at Birkenshaw (106 yards) and Gildersome (156 yards). Heaviest traffic was coal from Adwalton field to supply Bradford.

Powers for the extension to Ardsley were granted to the LB&HJ on 10 July 1854, the same day that the

BW&L Act was passed. The 4½ mile section, also double track was opened on 10 October 1857. There was an intermediate station at Morley, latterly known as Morley Top which was almost directly above the LNWR tunnel and far more convenient for the town than the LNWR station at Morley Low. Tingley station first appeared in *Bradshaw* for May 1859.

Through carriages between Kings Cross and Bradford began to be worked via Gildersome from 1 December 1857.

A branch to Ossett was authorised by the BW&L Act of 23 July 1860. A single line opened for coal traffic as far as Roundwood Colliery on 6 January 1862. On 7 April the line reached Flushdyke which was known as Ossett for the next two years whilst it remained the terminus. Ossett itself opened on 7 April 1864.

In 1861 both the LB&HJ and the BW&L obtained Acts allowing them to extend and meet one another at Batley. The LB&HJ opened from Adwalton Junction to Upper Batley on 19 August 1863 reaching Batley itself on 1 November 1864. The station at Upper Batley was only a temporary structure. It was moved to Howden Clough in 1866, allowing a station to open there on 1 November following completion of the permanent facilities at Upper Batley.

2-6-4T No 42639 pilots B1 No 61013 on the 8.52 (SO) Bradford to Cleethorpes seen rounding the curve between Laisterdyke and Cutlers Junction on 1 August 1964. *(M. Mitchell)*

Fowler 2-6-4T No 42411 passing Dudley Hill with the Bradford portion of a train from Kings Cross about 1964. *(H. Malham)*

A Fowler tank heads the 1.23pm, Bradford to Kings Cross between Dudley Hill and Birkenshaw on 10 August 1960. To the left are the earthworks of the curve which was never laid to join the Low Moor line.

(M. Mitchell)

The BW&L reached Batley from the other direction on 15 December 1864. The track was single. There were seven overbridges, nine underbridges and short tunnels at Chickenley Heath (47 yards) and Shaw Cross (209 yards). There was no intermediate station until Chickenley Heath opened on 2 July 1877.

The Dewsbury Loop

So far, the Wakefield-Batley-Bradford line had missed Dewsbury. Powers for a branch were granted to the Great Northern Railway in July 1871. It was to leave the existing Wakefield to Batley line at Runtlings Lane Junction. It included a 179 yard tunnel at Earlsheaton, four overbridges and three underbridges. The steepest gradient was 1 in 53. It opened to goods on 1 May 1874 and to passengers on 9 September with a service of 14 trains each way (five on Sundays) between Wakefield Westgate and Dewsbury.

On 1 May 1876 a north to west curve was opened at Wrenthorpe permitting a through service from Leeds Central to Dewsbury of six trains weekdays and three Sundays. The track from Wrenthorpe to Runtlings Lane Junction had been doubled by August 1873. The line in to Dewsbury was double from its opening.

Powers to extend to Batley were allowed to lapse but were then revived in 1877. The link was finally opened on 12 April 1880. From the previous temporary Dewsbury station, it passed through a 213-yard tunnel to reach a new island platform station at Dewsbury Central. Between there and Batley it crossed twice under the LNWR mainline. In all there were six overbridges and five under. The steepest gradient was 1 in 53. At Batley, an island platform was provided on the east side of the LNWR station. Most through traffic was diverted off the Chickenley Heath line onto the Dewsbury route.

Passenger trains were withdrawn completely from the Chickenley Heath line in July 1909 having latterly been worked by a railmotor four times per day each way. The previous November, the Dewsbury & Ossett Tramway had opened with a frequent service passing Chickenley Heath Station. The Great Northern Railway had objected, unsuccessfully, to the Tramway Order on the grounds of the adequacy of their own service, the weakness of the road overbridge at Chickenley Heath upon which the tramway would be laid and the possibility that the electric current might interfere with the Railway's signalling and telegraph systems.

Bradford to Wakefield in 1910

The service begins with the 5.02am all stations from Laisterdyke to Wakefield Kirkgate via Ardsley. There is a 5.37am all stations from Batley to Wakefield Westgate which has come from Leeds Central via Beeston. The first departure from Bradford

26

Dudley Hill saw occasional use by excursions after closure in 1952 but was rather derelict by 1966 when this 2-6-4T passed through with the Bradford portion of a train for Kings Cross. *(D.J. Mitchell)*

A Fairburn tank is brought to a stand at Birkenshaw box as it heads a Bradford to London train at Whit 1966.
(D.J. Mitchell)

B1 4-6-0 No 61033 'Dibatag' on a Bradford to Wakefield service at Drighlington in May 1952.
(B.G. Tweed/N.E. Stead Collection)

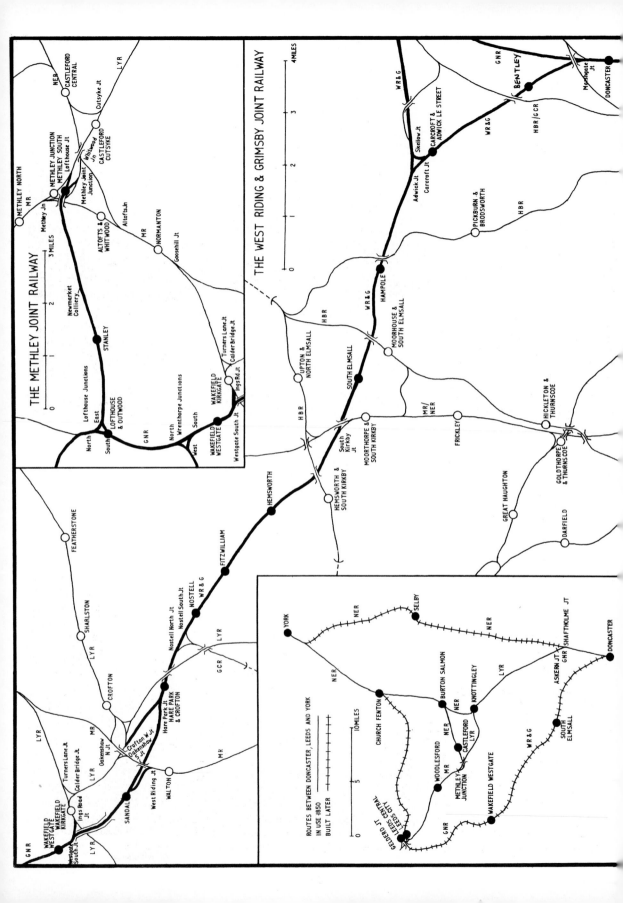

THE METHLEY JOINT RAILWAY

THE WEST RIDING & GRIMSBY JOINT RAILWAY

ROUTES BETWEEN DONCASTER, LEEDS AND YORK

IN USE 1850

BUILT LATER

J50 No 68935 heads past the closed station at Gildersome on 16 July 1963. *(M. Mitchell)*

J39 0-6-0 No 64760 passing Tingley with an afternoon freight in the Ardsley direction on 10 August 1962.
(M. Mitchell)

Great Northern 0-6-0 No 386 shunting at Morley Top. The engine was built in 1855 and withdrawn in 1902.
(D.J. Mitchell Collection)

J50 0-6-0T No 68915 climbing the 1 in 73/109 through Tingley with a transfer freight from Ardsley towards Morley Top in 1957. *(A.M. Ross)*

Tingley booking office in 1961, after closure.
(Peter E. Baughan)

Looking north at Ardsley in August 1960. A coal train waits to come off the Gildersome line. The M62 now crosses at this point. *(M. Mitchell)*

Exchange is the 5.37am all stations to Wakefield Kirkgate via Dewsbury. This gives a connection at Drighlington into a 6.13 all stations to Ardsley.

The pattern is repeated throughout the day right up to the 11.18pm Bradford Exchange to Wakefield Kirkgate via Dewsbury. There is no regularity to the service but most stations are served at least once an hour. There are quite a number of trains starting from Drighlington, generally giving a connection for Ardsley out of a Bradford-Dewsbury-Wakefield train or vice versa. In some instances, both trains continue to Wakefield.

There is a Mondays only 6.07am from Bradford Exchange to Kings Cross which joins the Leeds portion, also Mondays only, at Wakefield Westgate and then appears to be joined onto a Nottingham-London train at Grantham. It gives an arrival in Kings Cross at 10.40, some 50 minutes before the daily first through train from Bradford.

The 6.07 stops at St Dunstans, Laisterdyke and Ardsley. It also has conditional stops at Dudley Hill and Gildersome 'to take up for London' and at Birkenshaw and Morley 'to take up for Doncaster and south thereof'.

The 7.25am Bradford Exchange to Kings Cross stops at St Dunstans, Batley, Dewsbury Central and Ossett. It also stops conditionally at Laisterdayke, Birkenshaw, Upper Batley and Earlsheaton 'to take up for London'. At Wakefield Westgate it joined the 'Breakfast Car Express' which left Leeds Central at 7.50am. There were similar London through carriages during the rest of the day.

On Sundays the service was more restricted with just eight trains from Bradford to Wakefield, most frequent in the evening. Five went via Dewsbury and three via Ardsley.

Shaw Cross Tunnel on the Chickenley Heath branch in 1951. The track looks a bit rough. *(D. Ibbotson)*

Decline and Closure

The few remaining trains via Ardsley were withdrawn when diesel multiple units took over the majority of Bradford to Wakefield workings in February 1957. With stops at all the remaining open stations: Laisterdyke, Drighlington, Batley, Dewsbury Central and Ossett, the diesels gave an enhanced service at almost hourly intervals and cut the journey time from about 45 to 40 minutes to Wakefield Westgate. They didn't run on Sundays. From the following year, some journeys were extended through to Goole. The majority of Bradford to London trains still ran via Ardsley, one or two of them stopping at Morley Top until it closed in 1960.

During the 1950s and early '60s, there was a practice involving piecemeal closure of intermediate stations. The business was rather haphazard. Some of the closed stations continued to open specifically for seaside excursion trains until that class of traffic was abandoned soon after publication of the Beeching Report in 1963.

Between Bradford and Wakefield via Ardsley there were ten intermediate stations. These closed on ten different dates starting with Dudley Hill on 5 April 1952 and finishing with Laisterdyke on 2 July 1966.

Between Drighlington and Wakefield via Dewsbury, there were nine intermediate stations. Flushdyke had closed in 1941 whilst Batley is still open. The other seven closed on six different dates, none of them duplicating the ten in the previous paragraph. Batley Carr was first to go on 4 March 1950. Last were Dewsbury Central and Ossett which both closed on 5 September 1964, the day that the Bradford-Wakefield local service fell victim to the Beeching Report.

Complete closure followed in February 1965 between Adwalton Junction, near Drighlington, and Wrenthorpe, north of Wakefield except that access remained from Wrenthorpe South Junction to Roundwood Colliery until the end of October 1965.

Bradford portions of some Leeds-London trains continued to reach Wakefield via Drighlington and Ardsley until the summer of 1966 when they were diverted via Wortley. Closure to goods traffic soon followed and the through route was broken between Birkenshaw and Gildersome in October 1966. The remaining sections then closed as their remnants of freight business dried up. Last to go was an occasional wagon of steel over a single track between Laisterdyke and Dudley Hill which expired in 1981.

Tom Chapman, born about 1903, was a signalman at Howden Clough in the early 1930s. He bequeathed a photograph album which has been made available by his widow, Mrs Annie Chapman via her nephew Ian Stringer. Unfortunately, the album contains only small format prints, many of them faded. The negatives were lost in the depth of time. None the less, the reproductions on this and the next page reveal something of contemporary life at Howden Clough.

Two photographs taken at the start of a blizzard in February 1933. (Above) looking up the line towards Drighlington. (Right) view from the signal box across the Main line into the goods yard.

(Tom Chapman)

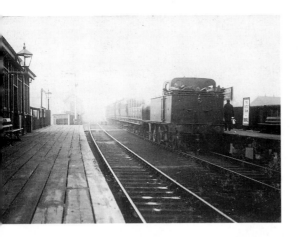

Anti clockwise from top left: An Ivatt 4-4-2T arrives at Howden Clough for Birstall with a Bradford to Wakefield stopping train in 1932: 4-4-2T No 4017 has temporarily abandoned its train opposite the signal box in order to detach cattle wagons: The enterprising staff have designed their own excursion publicity for the 1931 season: Self portrait at the lever frame in Howden Clough box. *(Tom Chapman)*

Seen from the derelict signal box, 61353 climbs through Howden Clough with the 12.00 Saturdays only
Lowestoft to Bradford on 29 August 1964. *(M. Mitchell)*

The 10.20 Kings Cross to Bradford crossing the LNWR 'Leeds New Line' at Howden Clough behind 61230
on 6 August 1960. *(M. Mitchell)*

J39 0-6-0 No 64907 restarts from Batley with the 2.18pm Kings Cross to Bradford Exchange on 16 July 1955.
(D. Holmes)

A similar view with a Wakefield to Bradford dmu pulling away from the Great Northern island platform. Only the LNWR main line (the double track to the right of the signal box) is still in use today.
(M. Mitchell)

Travelling in the opposite direction this class 111 twin powered Metro Cammell set has departed Batley for Dewsbury Central and Wakefield Westgate, July 1962.
(Peter Sunderland)

N1 0-6-2T No 69471 approaching Dewsbury Central from Wakefield about 1955. Dewsbury Junction signal box is just visible between the engine and the signal post. *(A.M. Ross)*

Earlsheaton station looking towards Dewsbury.
(A.M. Ross Collection)

B1 4-6-0 No 61229 passing Earlsheaton in June 1957 with the 4.47pm through coaches from Bradford Exchange to Kings Cross. *(A.M. Ross)*

J39 0-6-0 No 64801 passing Runtlings Lane Junction with Bradford to Kings Cross through coaches in 1954. *(A.M. Ross)*

J50 0-6-0T No 68916 attacks the 1 in 50 grade between Batley and Shaw Cross with the Wrenthorpe pick up in 1954.

(A.M. Ross)

The island platform station at Ossett looking towards Dewsbury in 1961.

(Peter E. Baughan)

N1 0-6-2T No 69453 rounds the curve between Wrenthorpe West and South Junctions with a local from Bradford to Wakefield via Dewsbury. *(G.M. Staddon/N.E. Stead Collection)*

B1 4-6-0 No 61013 'Topi' pulling away from Wakefield Westgate with a Cleethorpes to Bradford Exchange working on 9 July 1966. *(N.E. Stead)*

The Queensbury Lines

N1 0-6-2T No 69467 passing Queensbury with the 4.50pm Keighley to Halifax on 14 May 1955. For the last five years of the service, the handful of direct trains on this side of the triangle did not stop at Queensbury. *(John Oxley)*

To the west of the existing Bradford-Halifax line, the lie of the land becomes much more difficult, the plateau at over 1,000 feet being broken by steep sided valleys. The town of Queensbury stands at 1,150 feet. Assisted by supplies of local coal, the weaving industry flourished here, the best known firm being John Foster & Sons at Black Dyke Mills. Another high lying woollen township is Denholme at almost 1,000 feet. It was through this difficult territory that the Great Northern Railway drove its lines from Bradford to Halifax and Keighley.

The Halifax & Ovenden Junction Railway

Halifax Station is located at the bottom of the town. Both the Lancashire & Yorkshire and Great Northern Railways were concerned about the difficulty of transporting goods to the higher lying districts as well as congestion at the station itself. A possible solution to both problems lay in a branch line up the Ovenden Valley from where a good deal of traffic was being carted by road to Halifax Station.

The Halifax & Ovenden Junction Railway was incorporated on 30 June 1864 to run 2³/4 miles from just outside Halifax Station to Holmfield. The L&Y and GNR were each to subscribe one third of the

cost and would work the line jointly. Completion had to be within five years. Extensions of time were granted by Parliament in 1867 and 1870. The 1867 Act doubled the authorised capital whilst that of 1870 vested the line jointly in the two main line companies who were empowered to purchase the minority shareholdings. Preliminary work involved demolition of property to make the way for the viaduct between Halifax and North Bridge and construction of a new road bridge at the latter point with adequate clearance for the railway.

Opening to goods traffic was finally achieved on 17 August 1874 as far as North Bridge and to Holmfield two weeks later on Tuesday 1 September.

The Bradford & Thornton Railway

Separate proposals for a branch line to Thornton were advanced in 1865 by the Lancashire & Yorkshire and Great Northern Railways. The two then agreed to amalgamate their plans and to build the line jointly but no Act was obtained and the proposal failed.

Business interests in the locality, frustrated at the inaction of the main line companies, promoted the independent Bradford & Thornton Railway in 1870.

69471 pauses at North Bridge with the 6.45pm Halifax to Keighley on 21 May 1955.
(J.C.W. Halliday)

A class N1 tank pauses at Ovenden with a local to either Bradford or Keighley comprising two clerestory coaches.
(Martin Bairstow Collection)

69464 at Ovenden with the 3.32pm Bradford Exchange to Halifax on 14 May 1955. Also, caught on camera is our friend John Halliday who has just taken the photograph on page 86.
(John Oxley)

The line was to pass as close as possible to Queensbury where John Foster & Sons, of Black Dyke Mills, were amongst the promoters. In evidence to Parliament, they expressed the fear that local supplies of coal were going to run out and pointed to the difficulty of transporting coal by road from the nearest existing railway.

The Bradford & Thornton scheme drew support from the Great Northern who agreed to subscribe half the cost. Despite opposition from the Lancashire & Yorkshire Railway, it was authorised by an Act of 24 July 1871. The line was to commence at a triangular junction with the recently opened link between Hammerton Street and Bradford Exchange and was to run 5½ miles to Thornton. The 1¼ mile City Road goods branch was authorised by the same Act to give better access to the many mills in that part of Bradford.

By a further Act of 18 July 1872 the Bradford & Thornton project was fully absorbed by the Great Northern Railway. The earth works were heavy and construction took six years. The first opening, on 4 December 1876 was to goods traffic only as far as Great Horton and City Road. Extension to Clayton followed in July 1877 and to Thornton, after completion of Clayton Tunnel and Thornton Viaduct, on 1 May 1878.

The line opened to passengers on 14 October 1878 with five trains each weekday from Bradford Exchange to Thornton and two from Laisterdyke. The frequency from Bradford was soon increased but the through trains from Laisterdyke were shortlived. Convenient connections from Leeds became available with the opening of St Dunstans Station which first appeared in 'Bradshaw' for Thornton trains only in January 1879 and for the Leeds line in the following May edition.

The Halifax, Thornton & Keighley Railway
In 1864 an unsuccessful bid was made to promote a railway between Huddersfield, Halifax and Keighley. This would have offered a shorter route between Huddersfield and Halifax, a more central station at the latter place and a connection with the Midland Railway at Keighley. The promoters made a second attempt in 1867 gaining support of the Midland Railway for passage of a Bill through the House of Commons. The Midland then withdrew support in the Lords and the Bill was lost. In 1872 the Midland was again approached but declined support advising the promoters to press ahead on their own. Instead, they tried the Great Northern which expressed no interest in Huddersfield but offered to take up the Halifax to Keighley proposal if half the cost could be raised locally.

The Halifax, Thornton & Keighley Act was passed on 5 August 1873 despite the almost inevitable opposition of the Midland and Lancashire & Yorkshire Railways. The Midland tried to win over supporters of the Bill by promising to revive the earlier Huddersfield, Halifax & Keighley project. In November 1873 it deposited a Bill for a line from Huddersfield via a central station in Halifax then passing west of Queensbury to a triangular junction between Manningham and Bradford. The Bill failed

Cullingworth looking towards Keighley in 1957, two years after closure to passengers. *(J.C.W. Halliday)*

A J50 'Ardsley tank' entering Queensbury Tunnel, north portal, in the 1930s. (D. Ibbotson)

to make any progress.

The authorised Great Northern route utilised the almost complete Halifax & Ovenden Junction line as well as a part of the Bradford & Thornton which it was to join by a triangular junction at Queensbury. At Keighley the new line was to have an independent terminus close to the Midland Station. Connection between the two railways was 3/4 mile back towards Ingrow at what became Keighley GN Junction. In 1881 it was agreed that passenger trains would not run to the GNR terminus but would cross over on to the Midland and use a new joint station with separate platforms for GNR and Worth Valley branch trains. This opened on 6 May 1883. The section of line from GN Junction to Keighley Station was substantially rebuilt and the track doubled.

The route between Holmfield and Queensbury required the excavation of Strines Cutting and the boring of Queensbury Tunnel. Together these occupied most of the 2¼ mile stretch of line. Difficulties arose with water bearing strata but they were overcome in time for goods traffic to begin on 14 October 1878, the same day that Thornton opened to passengers. A station was opened at Queensbury on Easter Saturday 1879. Passenger trains began to run from Bradford to Halifax on 1 December 1879. Initially they ran non-stop after Queensbury but a temporary station was provided

at Holmfield within a fortnight. North Bridge opened on 25 March 1880. At first there were no plans for a station at Ovenden but local pressure met with success in June 1881.

The Halifax to Holmfield section remained in joint ownership with the Lancashire & Yorkshire Railway. Both companies ran goods trains but the Great Northern alone provided the passenger service.

Progress between Thornton and Keighley was slow. It was not until 1 September 1882 that a single line was available for goods traffic as far as Denholme which saw its first passengers on 1 January 1884. The line opened to Keighley goods depot on 1 April but the junction with the Midland Railway was still not ready. As an interim measure eight passenger trains per day were extended to Ingrow from Monday 7 April. Finally, on 1 November 1884, the Great Northern began to serve Keighley passenger station with 18 departures on weekdays and four on Sundays. Evidence that the Great Northern Railway had finally arrived came with the advertising of cheap excursions to Lincoln, Boston and Skegness.

The line passed no nearer than within two miles of Wilsden but a station opened with that name on 1 July 1886 after an approach road had been built from the nearby tiny village of Harecroft. The question of a station at Cross Roads was raised but nothing ever happened. The village stands above Lees Moor Tunnel and a station would have had to be sited at the Ingrow end overlooking the Worth Valley. Apparently the Great Northern thought that it might pick up a bit of traffic for Haworth but not enough to tempt them into providing a station there.

Queensbury Station

Situated at the focal point of the Great Northern lines between Bradford, Halifax and Keighley, this station was renowned not only for its unusual construction but for its remoteness. The town of Queensbury could claim to be the most important along the route. Its principal industrialists had supported the construction of the railway and had influenced the route from Bradford to Thornton so as to pass as close as practical to Queensbury. The distance from the town to the station was one mile and the difference in altitude about 400 feet. Prior to the advent of motor transport this would have been insufficient an obstacle to have prevented rail traffic developing. The complaints against the Great Northern Railway by the inhabitants of Queensbury did not arise from the location of the station because they probably accepted that it had to be on the railway line. When the line opened in 1878 there was no station at Queensbury until a temporary structure was thrown together for Easter 1879. This had no goods facilities, no access for vehicles and the only footpath was unmade and unlit.

On 3 January 1882, the Queensbury Local Board asked the Great Northern Railway what it proposed to do on the question of road access to the station. The Company replied that alterations to the station might be required when the line to Keighley opened and proposed that action be deferred. The Local Board asked that, as an interim measure, the footpath should be provided with gas lamps. The Railway replied in April that there was no urgency for this now that it was summer. On 5 September the Local Board pointed out that it would soon be winter again. A year later some lights had been provided but local opinion doubted whether they were enough. In February 1884 the Great Northern Railway proposed a road from the town to the station and subsequently asked the Local Board to contribute to the cost. The Queensbury Local Board replied that they would not spend ratepayers' money on a road which only led to a railway station and which for the greater part of its length lay outside the Queensbury district boundary. They informed the railway 'That the inhabitants of this locality are very indignant at the treatment they have hitherto received from the Great Northern Company for, while other villages on the route are provided with good roads to the station, Queensbury is entirely neglected although it should be the most important'.

This dialogue continued for several more years but the Great Northern Railway was not entirely inactive. In 1885 an engineers' report showed that it would be possible to construct a new station with platforms on all three sides of the triangular junction. As for communication with the town two alternative forms of rail link were discussed. The cheapest alternative was for a rope-worked incline at a gradient of 1 in 6. a more satisfactory alternative but at double the cost was a circuitous route, two miles in length with a maximum gradient of 1 in 30. In 1888 the Great Northern Board resolved to press ahead with the latter idea if half the cost could be raised locally. John Foster & Sons, who favoured the circuitous locomotive worked line, advised that trade was bad and went on to blame the lack of railway facilities for this.

Work commenced on the new station in 1889 and a road to the town was included in the plans. The station opened on 1 January 1890 and the road came into use soon afterwards. No action was taken on the question of a branch line but sidings were provided. In 1895 consideration was given to the suitability of Briggs' tramway for connection to and use by the railways. This was a track used for rope-hauling coal from the mine near Queensbury station to the town. No action was taken. On 17 February 1896, the Great Northern directors visited Queensbury and soon afterwards a few more lights were provided on Station Road and poster boards erected at the top of the road together with a signpost in the form of a hand pointing to the station. These appear to have represented the ultimate in Queensbury's railway facilities! In 1901 electric tramways were opened to the centre of the town from both Bradford and Halifax and soon began to make inroads into Great Northern passenger traffic.

Train services

Until the British Railways period it was often difficult to differentiate between through trains and connections in the public timetable. This means that it is practically impossible to tell whether a train from Bradford Exchange ran through to Halifax with a connection for Keighley or whether the train ran to Keighley with a connection for Halifax. My grandparents, occasional passengers between Horton Park and Halifax, told me that they used to see which way the train turned at Queensbury then act accordingly. At certain times of the day trains stood on all three sides of the triangle allowing connections to be made in all directions. For example, the 1910 timetable shows arrivals at 10.26, 10.30 and 10.31a.m. from Bradford Exchange, Halifax and Keighley followed by departures at 10.33 to Keighley, 10.35 to Bradford Exchange and 10.36 to Halifax.

At that time there were 22 weekday departures from Bradford Exchange to Halifax or Keighley. In most cases the other of these places could be reached by changing at Queensbury. There were 21 trains from Halifax for the Queensbury line and 16 starting from Keighley. On Sundays nine trains left Bradford Exchange for Halifax or Keighley. The journey from Bradford to Halifax by this route took between 35 and 40 minutes depending on the number of stops and the duration of the wait at Queensbury. This was slower than by the alternative

WEEKDAYS

		A am	B am	A am	A am	A am	B am	A am	A pm	B pm	A pm	B pm	A pm	A pm	B pm	B pm	A pm	A pm	pm	pm	B pm	A pm
BRADFORD EXCHANGE	dep	5 45	5 55	6 30	7 15	7 54	9 03	10 08	12 10	12 50	1 30		3 30	4 38	5 15	5 45	6 00	6 46	—	9 15	10 27	11 20
ST DUNSTANS		5 49	5 58	6 35	7 20	7 58	9 06	10 11	12 13	12 53	1 36		3 34	4 41	5 18	5 48		6 49	—	9 19	—	—
HORTON PARK		5 53	6 03	6 39	7 24	8 02	9 10	10 15	12 17	12 57	1 40		3 38	4 45	5 22	5 52	6 06	6 53	—		—	—
GREAT HORTON		5 56	6 07	6 42	7 27	8 05	9 13	10 18	12 20	1 00	1 43		3 41	4 48	5 25	5 55	6 09	6 56	—	9 25	10 34	—
CLAYTON		6 00	6 12	6 46	7 31	8 09	9 17	10 22	12 24	1 04	1 47		3 45	4 52	5 29	5 59	6 13	7 00	—	9 29	10 38	—
QUEENSBURY	arr	6 04	6 17	6 50	7 35	8 13	9 21	10 26	12 28	1 08	1 51		3 49	4 56	5 33	6 03	6 17	7 04	—	9 33	10 42	—
QUEENSBURY	dep	—	6 18	6N55	—	8N18	9 25	10N35	12 29		1 52	3N54	5N00	5 37	6 07	—	—	—	—	10 49		
THORNTON		—	6 22	9 59		8 22	9 29	10 39	12 33		1 56	3 58	5 04	5 41	6 11	—	—	—	—	10 53		
DENHOLME		—	6 25	7 02		8 25	9 32	10 42	12 36		1 59	4 01	5 07	5 44	6 14	—	—	—	—	10 56		
WILSDEN		—	6 28	7 05		8 28	9 35	10 45	12 39		2 02	4 05	5 10	5 47	6 17	—	—	—	—	10 59		
CULLINGWORTH		—	6 32	7 09		8 31	9 38	10 48	12 42		2 05	4 07	5 13	5 50	6 20	—	—	—	—	11 02		
INGROW		—	6 39	7 16		8 38	9 45	10 55	12 49		2 12	4 14	5 20	5 57	6 27	—	—	—	—	11 09		
KEIGHLEY	arr	—	6 42	7 19		8 41	9 48	10 58	12 52		2 15	4 17	5 23	6 00	6 30	—	—	—	—	11 12		
QUEENSBURY	dep	6 07		6 58	7 38	8 15	9N26	10 34	12N32	15		3 52	5 04	5N37		6 18	7 08	8N08	9 37	10N51		
HOLMFIELD		6 11	—	7 02	7 42	8 19	9 30	10 38	12 36	19		3 56	5 10	5 41	—	6 22	7 12	8 12	9 41	10 55		
OVENDEN		6 13	—	7 04	7 44	8 21	9 32	10 40	12 38	21		3 58	5 12	5 43	—	6 24	7 14	8 14	9 43	10 57		
NORTH BRIDGE		6 17	—	7 08	7 48	8 25	9 36	10 44	12 42	25		4 02	5 16	5 47	—	6 28	7 18	8 18	9 47	11 01		
HALIFAX	arr	6 19	—	7 10	7 50	8 27	9 38	10 46	12 44	27		4 04	5 18	5 49	—	6 30	7 20	8 20	9 49	11 03	11 43	

WEEKDAYS

		A am	B am	B am	A am	B am	B am	A pm	B pm	A pm	B pm	A pm	B pm	A pm	B pm	A pm			B pm	B pm	A pm	A pm
HALIFAX	dep	6N35	—	7N50	8 20	9 05	10N12	12 03		1 17		3N35	4N41	5 10	5 43	—		—	7 50	10 25		
NORTH BRIDGE		6 38	—	7 53	8 23	9 08	10 15	12 06		1 20		3 38	4 44	5 13	5 46	—		—	7 53	10 28		
OVENDEN		6 42	—	7 57	8 27	9 12	10 19	12 10		1 24		3 42	4 48	5 17	5 50	—		—	7 57	10 32		
HOLMFIELD		6 45	—	8 00	8 30	9 15	10 22	12 13		1 27		3 45	4 51	5 20	5 53	—		—	8 00	10 35		
QUEENSBURY	arr	6 51	—	8 06	8 36	9 21	10 28	12 19		1 33		3 51	4 57	5 26	5 59	—		—	8 06	10 41		
KEIGHLEY	dep	6 25	7 05	7 37	—	8N52	10 07	11N50	12 42	—	1 41	3 18	4 28	4N55	—			5 46	6 31	7N27	10N15	
INGROW		6 31	7 11	7 43	—	8 58	10 07	11 56	12 48	—	1 47	3 24	4 34	5 01	—			5 52	6 37	7 33	10 21	
CULLINGWORTH		6 39	7 19	7 51	—	9 06	10 15	12 04	12 56	—	1 55	3 32	4 42	5 09	—			6 01	6 45	7 41	10 29	
WILSDEN		6 43	7 23	7 55	—	9 10	10 19	12 08	1 00	—	1 59	3 36	4 46	5 13	—			6 05	6 49	7 45	10 34	
DENHOLME		6 46	7 26	7 58	—	9 13	10 22	12 11	1 03	—	2 02	3 39	4 49	5 16	—			6 08	6 52	7 48	10 37	
THORNTON		6 50	7 30	8 02	—	9 17	10 26	12 15	1 07	—	2 06	3 43	4 53	5 20	—			6 12	6 56	7 52	10 41	
QUEENSBURY	arr	6 53	7 33	8 05	—	9 20	10 29	12 18	1 10	—	2 09	3 46	4 56	5 23	—			6 15	6 59	7 55	10 44	
QUEENSBURY	dep	6 59	7 34	8 10	8 37	9 25	10 32	12 22		16	35	2 11	3 56	5 03	5 27	6 00		6 17	7 07	8 09	10 50	
CLAYTON		7 02	7 37	8 13	8 40	9 28		12 25		19	38	2 14	3 59	5 07	5 30	6 03		6 20	7 10	8 12	10 53	
GREAT HORTON		7 05	7 40	8 16	8 43		10 38	12 28		22	41	2 17	4 02	5 10	5 33	6 06		6 23	7 13	8 15	10 56	
HORTON PARK		7 07	7 42	8 18	8 45		10 40	12 30		24	43	2 19	4 04	5 12	5 35	6 08		6 25	7 15	8 17	—	
ST DUNSTANS		7 11	7 46	8 22	8 49		10 44	12 34		28	47	2 23	4 08	5 16	5 39	6 12		6 30	7 19	8 21	—	
BRADFORD EXCHANGE	arr	7 14	7 49	8 25	8 52	9 37	10 47	12 37		31	50	2 26	4 12	5 19	5 42	6 15		6 35	7 22	8 24	11 04	

NO SUNDAY SERVICE

A – Through train between BRADFORD EXCHANGE and HALIFAX
B – Through train between BRADFORD EXCHANGE and KEIGHLEY
N – Through train between KEIGHLEY and HALIFAX

JULY 1947

69434 pulling away from Great Horton with the 5.47pm Bradford Exchange to Keighley on 14 May 1955.

(J.C.W. Halliday)

Denholme looking towards Keighley in 1957. Passenger access had been via the footbridge and staircase.
(J.C.W. Halliday)

Lancashire & Yorkshire service which was more frequent. A Great Northern train from Bradford to Keighley took 45 minutes, twice as long as the faster trains by the Midland Railway from Forster Square.

Whilst the railways held a monopoly over the available traffic the Queensbury lines prospered, despite their disadvantages against the older railways and the inconvenient location of some of the stations. Some traffic was lost to the electric tramways after the turn of the century. The Bradford trams began to eat into the traffic at stations as far as Thornton, whilst Ovenden, Holmfield and Queensbury became prey to the Halifax tramways. Because of the breaks of gauge, trams were not a threat on longer journeys in the West Riding. Later on, buses were to prove a different proposition.

Decline and Closure
Sunday trains were withdrawn in December 1938 but otherwise the timetable held up reasonably well. The one reproduced for Summer 1947 is superior to the 'austerity' service suffered by many neighbouring lines. In 1950 the timetable was recast to give a better peak hour service to and from Bradford but with fewer off peak trains and a reduction in direct trains between Halifax and Keighley.

St Dunstans and Horton Park Stations closed in September 1952. Less than three years later, the entire passenger service was withdrawn. According to 'official figures' given in the House of Commons, the cost of running the trains was seven times the revenue and an average of only three passengers joined each train at each of the eleven intermediate stations remaining on the line.

Goods and occasional excursions continued for the next 12 months with the line still being open on two shifts. Then, in May 1956 the sections between Queensbury and Holmfield and between Cullingworth and Ingrow were closed to all traffic. This saved the cost of maintaining Queensbury and Lees Moor Tunnels and divided the route into three separate branch lines which were then operated with reduced signalling. Between Horton Park and Cullingworth, a travelling signalman rode on the train in order to open up the signal boxes for access to the various goods yards.

The remaining operation was progressively cut back over the next 18 years. Holmfield and the High Level closed in 1960, Cullingworth in 1963, Thornton and Ingrow in 1965. The last remnants were from St Dunstans to Horton Park and City Road which survived until 1972 and Halifax to North Bridge coal yard which disappeared two years after that.

Much of the line has since been redeveloped. A school has been built on the site of Thornton Station. The railway has been used to create a pedestrian underpass at Manchester Road. Thornton. Hewenden and Cullingworth Viaducts survive as monuments to this once impressive railway.

The 'Closure' Controversy
I don't actually think that there was one. Although the closure had been known about for some time, it took until Friday 20 May 1955, for somebody to organise a protest meeting at Harecroft near Wilsden Station. This attracted a bit of publicity not least because it fell in the last week of a General Election campaign and was attended by no fewer

than five candidates, some of them destined to be successful, who all pledged themselves to oppose the closure which duly took place the following day.

The *Halifax Courier* (Saturday 21 May 1955) was very dismissive of the protests. It suggested that they should have done something sooner if the railway really was 'chock-a-block with factory and engineering shopworkers and schoolchildren . . . an indispensable link with places of employment and all in all a flourishing section of British Railways'. The paper noted that the matter had been 'scarcely discussed' by Halifax Council. It went on to suggest that British Railways 'is not so lacking in business ability as not to have examined all ways and means – including running diesel cars – of keeping the line open'.

The quality of argument by both sides was not very advanced. Opponents of closure saw possible salvation in diesel multiple units, which had revived the Bradford Exchange to Leeds Central service so successfully since June 1954. The BR response to that included 'no potential', 'lack of available diesels' (both plausible arguments) and 'gradients too steep' (absolute nonsense). Some protestors claimed that recent passenger figures were artificially low so the Transport Users Consultative Committee ought to have based its decision on pre-War loadings. BR cited the condition of certain structures as a reason for closure (plausible without major expenditure) and the 1947 coal crisis (whatever that had to do with it).

Over the next few months, the main argument in favour of reopening seems to have been the continued use of the line for goods traffic, excursions and dmu driver training. This was answered when the through route was severed in May 1956.

A few people did manage to keep the subject alive occasionally hitting the headlines. On 16 December 1955, the MP for Shipley initiated a House of Commons debate on a motion, supported by other local members, calling for reinstatement of the passenger service. *Trains Illustrated* (February 1956) reported this under the heading 'Storm in the West Riding'. The article concluded that complete closure was more likely than passenger restoration which, it was claimed, would require the boring of a replacement 1½ mile tunnel at Queensbury.

The line featured again in *Trains Illustrated* (September 1957) under the heading 'Top Secret and Technical'. The subject was the test carried out on 18 July between Lees Moor Tunnel and Ingrow on the effect upon concrete sleepers of deliberately derailing class G5 No.67338.

The March 1958 issue reported another series of tests, this time of the effect of smoke and fumes produced inside Lees Moor Tunnel by class 20 diesels D8010 and D8011 and by class A3 No.60081 'Shotover'. On both occasions, the operations were attended by strict security. *Trains Illustrated* suggested that this might 'have at least as much, if not more, to do with incensed local feeling that a

branch satisfactory for experiments should be good enough for a regular service, as with any threat to the nation if the object of the trials leaked out.'

The late Bob Cryer contributed to the local press in 1960 suggesting that passenger services should be restored. Other people wrote in support but a BR spokesman said it was impossible as the stations didn't have gas for lighting nor water for the toilets. Apparently, staff were then sent immediately to cut off the gas and water supplies.

Bob Cryer subsequently wrote that his disappointment at the fate of the Queensbury lines determined him to ensure that 'the same fate of indifference and neglect' did not befall the adjacent Worth Valley branch. In 1962 he became the founder chairman of the Keighley & Worth Valley Railway Preservation Society.

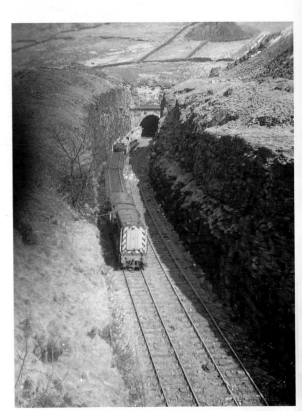

A Class 08 diesel passing through Strines Cutting in 1963 with tracks recovered from Queensbury Tunnel.
(D.J. Mitchell)

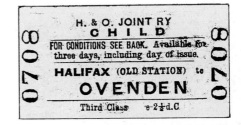

The Queensbury line platforms at St. Dunstans shortly before closure in 1952. *(Telegraph & Argus)*

The 7.40pm Keighley to Bradford Exchange entering Ingrow, on 21 May 1955. N1 No 69471 carries a headboard 'The Economist' on the buffer beam. *(Roy Brook)*

J39 0-6-0 No 64732 comes off the City Road branch at Horton Junction in 1956. *(Peter Sunderland)*

A 'Black Five' passing North Bridge Yard with the pick up goods for Holmfield and St. Pauls in June 1960.
(J.C.W. Halliday)

Class A3 4-6-2 No. 60081 'Shotover' passing Great Horton on its way back from the smoke tests in Lees Moor Tunnel on 11 January 1958. *(J.C.W. Halliday)*

A WD 2-8-0 and brake van about to enter Clayton Tunnel on their way back from Thornton about 1964. Only one track was then in use. *(D.J. Mitchell)*

69451 pauses at Great Horton with a train for Bradford Exchange. *(N.E. Stead Collection)*

WD 2-8-0 No 90711 returning from Thornton takes the Laisterdyke curve at St. Dunstans in 1965.
(D.J. Mitchell)

Thornton Station, two years after closure to passengers looking towards Bradford.
(J.C.W. Halliday)

The view from a carriage window as the 2.31pm Bradford Exchange to Keighley pauses at Denholme on 19 February 1955. Ahead is the 140 yard Doe Park Tunnel.
(John Oxley)

One of the eight pioneer Derby lightweight units 79004/79504 at Keighley on driver training over the Queensbury line in 1955.
(W.H. Foster, courtesy John Holroyd)

WITHDRAWAL OF PASSENGER TRAINS

Halifax—Bradford—Keighley
via Queensbury

As from the 23rd May, 1955, the passenger train service will be withdrawn from the Halifax—Bradford—Keighley, via Queensbury branches. The stations concerned are:—

CLAYTON	HALIFAX	WILSDEN
CULLINGWORTH	(North Bridge)	OVENDEN
DENHOLME	HOLMFIELD	QUEENSBURY
GREAT HORTON	INGROW	THORNTON
	(East)	

Queensbury, Denholme, Wilsden and Clayton stations will be converted to unstaffed public delivery sidings for freight traffic, and Ovenden station will be closed entirely.

NOTE.—The passenger train services Halifax—Bradford, via Low Moor and Bradford—Keighley, via Shipley, will continue as at present.

ALTERNATIVE FACILITIES

For Passengers

Bus services operated by the Hebble Motor Services Ltd., West Yorkshire Road Car Co. Ltd., Yorkshire Woollen District Transport Co. Ltd., West Riding Automobile Co. Ltd., and the Bradford and Halifax Corporations serve the area. Additional bus services will be run by the Hebble Motor Services serving the following places:—

(1) Clayton (Town Gate)   (2) Wilsden (New Inn)
    School Green Hotel   Harecroft (Station Road)
    Yews Green (Brow Lane)   Cullingworth (Mill Street)
    Queensbury (Stag's Head)

Particulars of these services with connecting times at Denholme, Halifax, Keighley, Bradford, etc., are shown on the following pages.

For Merchandise

By Passenger Train

The present facilities for parcels traffic, passengers' unaccompanied luggage, etc., will be maintained at Great Horton, Thornton, Cullingworth Ingrow East and Holmfield. At Clayton, Queensbury, Denholme, Wilsden, Ovenden and Halifax (North Bridge) collection and delivery services by railway motor vehicles will continue as at present. A small additional charge will be made for collection or delivery outside the normal boundary.

By Goods Train

Clayton, Denholme, Queensbury and Wilsden stations will be converted to public delivery sidings for goods train traffic in full truck loads.

Traffic may be loaded by arrangement as follows:—

For Loading at	Advise the Agent at	Telephone
Clayton	Great Horton	Bradford 72255
Denholme	Thornton	Thornton 3193
Queensbury	Thornton	Thornton 3193
Wilsden	Cullingworth	Cullingworth 8116

Traffic requiring collection or delivery by railway vehicle will be dealt with as at present.

The District Passenger Manager, Leeds (telephone Leeds 31711, extension 268) and the District Goods Manager, Leeds (telephone Leeds 31711, extension 240) or any Station Master in the area will provide further information on application or, if desired, arrangements will be made for a Railway Service Representative to call.

A WD 2-8-0 descending towards North Bridge with track recovered from further up the line.

(D.J. Mitchell)

The Halifax High Level Railway

The last passenger train to visit St. Pauls, a Stephenson Locomotive Society Special with Class N1 No 69430 on 6 September 1953.
(N. Bland)

The full name of the undertaking incorporated in 1884 was The Halifax High Level & North & South Junction Railway. It was authorised to build a total of 5¼ route miles from Holmfield serving Halifax with two branches – one to St Paul's and one to make end on connection with an extension of the Hull & Barnsley Railway at a Central Station in George Square, Halifax.

By this means, Anglo-Scottish expresses of the Midland Railway would be able to travel from Sheffield through Barnsley, Huddersfield, Halifax (Central) and over the GNR to Keighley. In the event, the Hull & Barnsley never quite reached Barnsley let alone Huddersfield or Halifax. By an Act of 1886, the Halifax High Level was restricted to the Holmfield to St Paul's route. Arrangements were confirmed whereby the line would be worked jointly by the Lancashire & Yorkshire and the Great Northern Railways – the latter always provided the passenger service.

The line opened for goods as far as Pellon on 1 August 1890 and to all traffic throughout five weeks later. The timetable was generally arranged so that the High Level train left St Paul's a minute or two before a Bradford train left Halifax Old thus arriving in the bay platform at Holmfield in time to allow passengers to change for Bradford. In 1910 there were 11 departures from St Paul's Mondays to Fridays, 12 Saturdays and five on Sundays. A steam railmotor was given a trial on the branch about 1906 but did not find favour, possibly because of the gradients.

The High Level Company was absorbed jointly by the L&Y and GN Railways by an Act of 1894 which compelled them to build a goods station at Wheatley. They resisted pressure for a passenger station there.

The branch was steeply graded and heavily engineered with an 810 yard tunnel at Wheatley, approached from both directions by deep cuttings. There was a ten arch viaduct across the Hebble Valley.

St Paul's and Pellon Stations served a well populated area of Halifax but the train service was of little value to anybody travelling (say) to Huddersfield or Manchester. By 1898 both St Paul's and Pellon were linked to Halifax Old Station by electric tramways. The High Level passenger service became one of the 'temporary' closures effected at the end of 1916 to help free railway staff for use as cannon fodder on the Western Front. It never resumed though there were occasional excursions during the 1920s and '30s. The track was singled and most of the signalling removed. Latterly it was worked as 'one engine in steam' from Holmfield to Pellon and with no block regulation thence to St Paul's. The engine shed at Holmfield was closed after the passenger service withdrawn.

The main value of the High Level line was for freight. St Paul's was at an altitude some 325 feet higher than the Old Station. A wagon of coal did not mind the circuitous journey via Holmfield. There were a lot of mills and factories in the upper part of Halifax and goods traffic continued until June 1960.

A Holmfield to St. Pauls train approaching Pellon.
(Martin Bairstow Collection)

A 'Black Five' shunting at Pellon during the final week of operation in June 1960.
(J.C.W. Halliday)

Wheatley Tunnel from the St. Pauls end in 1949.
(D. Ibbotson)

The Shipley Branch

It wasn't normally this busy at Shipley (GN). N1 0-6-2T No 69430 with the 'West Riding Rail Tour' in April 1953, 22 years after closure to normal passenger traffic. *(D. Ibbotson)*

The 6¼ mile branch was promoted by two independent companies. The Bradford, Eccleshill & Idle Railway was authorised in June 1866, the Idle & Shipley in August 1867. Both were supported by the GNR which subscribed capital and agreed to work the lines upon completion. The balance of capital could not be raised locally and with no progress on construction, the GNR took over the whole enterprise by an Act of 1871.

The branch began with a triangular junction at Laisterdyke East and Cutlers. It climbed gradually at first before descending into the Aire Valley. The last two miles were at 1 in 61. Col. Hutchinson, who inspected the line for the Board of Trade, recommended the use of continuous brakes. They later became mandatory for passenger trains but unfitted freight continued throughout the 90 years that this line was in operation. Shipley bound trains had to stop at Eccleshill to pin down the wagon brakes. On more than one occasion, trains did run away ending up in the road beyond the buffer stops at Shipley Station. 0-6-0ST No.601 managed this in 1883. Sister engine No.916 repeated the exploit on 18 May 1916.

The line, which was double track, opened to goods as far as Idle on 9 March 1874 and to Shipley on 4 May. Passenger trains began on 18 January 1875 with 13 each way on weekdays and five on Sundays, nearly all of them through from Bradford Exchange. At Shipley, there was a single platform terminus and fairly extensive goods depot adjacent to Leeds Junction (the present Shipley East Junction). On 1 November 1875 a double track connection was opened between the GN and Midland Systems.

In addition to passengers and general freight, the line carried limestone from Skipton direction to Bowling and Low Moor Ironworks. It carried coal from pits near Gildersome to Shipley and beyond and was used to despatch stone from Idle.

The passenger service suffered from the relatively indirect route. By 1901 electric trams were running from Bradford to Eccleshill, Idle and Thackley far more frequently than the trains.

Passenger trains were withdrawn at the end of January 1931. According to the *Telegraph & Argus,* one commuter from Eccleshill was so aggrieved that he had taken the extreme step (for those days) of writing to the Company. Occasional excursions continued but the line was reduced to single track with the signal boxes at Eccleshill and Idle abolished. The last passenger train to traverse the line was the RCTS 'West Riding Rail Tour' on 6 September 1964.

Closure to through traffic took place at the end of October 1964. A spur continued for another two years from Laisterdyke to just beyond Quarry Gap Junction. Shipley to Idle continued until October 1968. The main station buildings survive at both Thackley and Shipley. Both have been renovated within recent times, the former as a house, the latter in commercial use.

The last income derived by British Railways from Idle Station was a modest rent for the use of one room by the Bradford Railway Circle between 1965 and 1971. After losing their base at Manningham, the Circle moved into what was almost still a working station. By the time I joined them at the end of 1969, the track had been lifted and the place was getting derelict.

An Ivatt 2-6-0 shunting Idle goods yard 1965. *(D.J. Mitchell)*

B16 2-6-0 No 61268 climbing from Shipley towards Thackley in 1957. The Midland line to Leeds runs in front of the Valley Scouring Co. *(J.C.W. Halliday)*

Jubilee class 4-6-0 No 45565 'Victoria' climbing past the former Great Northern signal box at Shipley Junction.

J39 0-6-0 No 64907 passing Idle with a freight towards Laisterdyke. *(G. Townsend)*

Jubilee class 4-6-0 No 45694 'Bellerophon' climbing between Eccleshill and Quarry Gap with a mixed freight in 1964. *(H. Malham)*

Fairburn 2-6-4T No 42055 comes off the Shipley branch at Cutlers Junction about 1963. *(H. Malham)*

The Shipley Ledger

An impediment to the growth of passenger traffic on the Shipley branch was the separate station at Shipley. If trains had run to the Midland Station, they would have taken customers closer to the town centre and would have offered a range of connections. The only point in favour of the Great Northern Station was its proximity to the township of Windhill. If that was considered important, it would have been possible to provide an intermediate halt at Windhill between Shipley and Thackley.

These considerations may not have been important in 1875 but the arrangement could have been changed later on, possibly as an alternative to withdrawing the passenger service in 1931.

Once could envisage a circular service from Bradford Forster Square to Bradford Exchange or possible from Forster Square to Leeds via Idle and Pudsey. A lot of housing was built near the line between Idle and Eccleshill after the Second World War when the railway was still open for goods. A fair bit more has been built since complete closure including some on the former track bed.

Enough of speculation. We are able to look at the actual passenger business transacted at Shipley GN Station thanks to a ledger from the 1880s which is in the care of Bob Watson. The book is headed up as a weekly summary of 'foreign' passenger traffic but, with only four such tickets sold in a month, the Shipley Station Master has used it to record all passenger tickets sold.

Totals for the month of May 1882 are reproduced on page 66.

Third class is referred to in the ledger as 'Parliamentary' for which the usual fare, laid down by statute was one penny per mile. However the fare to Bradford Exchange (8¼ miles) is held down to 3d by the existence of the shorter Midland route. Similarly the fare to Leeds (14¾ miles) is restricted to 9d. It is actually 11 miles from Shipley to Leeds by the Midland but that fare in turn would be suppressed as the Midland couldn't charge more from Shipley to Leeds than from Bradford and that was held down by the shorter GN mileage via Stanningley.

The nineteenth century value of money was at least 100 times what it is today so 3d third class single to Bradford represents at least £1.25 and 9d single to Leeds some £3.75 at 1999 prices. Actual fares from Shipley in 1999 are Bradford 70p single £1.20 off peak return and Leeds £1.70 single, £1.80 off peak return.

The majority of bookings from Shipley (GN) station were to Thackley, Idle, Eccleshill and Laisterdyke, third class at fares not exceeding 3d single. This business would have been vulnerable to the more frequent electric trams which began in 1904.

The modest number of tickets to Bradford confirm that the shorter Midland route was getting most of the traffic. Perhaps there were just a few people from the Windhill area who found the Great Northern more convenient. 50 years later, in an obituary to the line, the Telegraph & Argus suggested that only courting couples would have travelled from Shipley to Bradford by the Great Northern – 25 minutes with a compartment to themselves.

Bookings to Leeds represent only one or two per day. Stanningley is the most popular destination requiring a change of train but that is only six or seven a day. There is no significant long distance traffic apart from an excursion to Skegness which has generated 15% of the month's revenue. The attraction of Skegness was it being a Great Northern destination.

97½ % of tickets are third class, 1½ % second and just 1% first. This underlines the farce of conveying three classes on all trains.

The Great Northern had included third class carriages on virtually all trains since 1872 after which second class travel declined sharply. It was abolished on the West Riding lines from 1 January 1886. Trains then conveyed just first and third class until the latter was renamed second in 1956.

In the following month of June 1882, the number of tickets sold rises to 9,903 but revenue is down to £133 6s. 3d.; More local journeys but no excursion to Skegness. A strange appearance in the June 1883 page is a full range of tickets, first, second and third class, single and return to Bradford Adolphus Street. All six variants begin at number 0000 and three of them remain there. They did, however, issue nine first class singles, 380 third singles and three third returns at fares identical to those applicable to Bradford Exchange. Tickets sold to Bradford Exchange are about the same as the previous month. There is no subsequent mention of Adlophus Street which had closed to passenger traffic in 1867. If they were using Adolphus Street because of capacity problems at Exchange or for any other temporary purpose, it seems odd that they should print a separate supply of tickets for this month only.

Revenue for July 1882 is up to £194 7s 3d thanks mainly to Skegness bookings and an excursion to Harrogate and Ripon. August and September are each over £170 but October is down to a mere £97 16s 4½ d from 6,789 tickets. November and December are even worse, with only two customers for Kings Cross (in two months) and none at all for Skegness.

The seasonal trend is repeated through 1883 with July delivering revenue of £297 18s 7½d, more than three times the base figure. This is largely explained by Salvation Army and Primitive Methodist trips to Scarborough which generated 430½ and 346 tickets respectively at 3 shillings each. There were also 17 excursion tickets sold at half a crown each to Dogdyke (Lincolnshire). This was one of the 'stations with evocative names' mentioned in The Slow Train by Flanders & Swann.

Commuters alight from a Bradford to Shipley train at Eccleshill about 1930.
(P.R. White Collection)

An N2 tank pauses at Idle en route from Bradford to Shipley shortly before closure in January 1931.
(P.R. White Collection)

Thackley Station looking towards Idle about 1910. The booking office, which survives as a private house, was at the top of the left hand ramp, behind the camera.
(Peter E. Baughan Collection)

July is also the peak month in 1884 with 12,559 tickets bringing in £298 16s 1d. This includes 263½ returns to Skegness and 499½ excursions to Grimsby.

They didn't do quite as well in July 1885 with only £238 9s 9d. The most popular excursion destinations that summer being 352½ tickets for Scarborough, 207 for Skegness, 83½ for Grimsby and a creditable 26½ for Dogdyke.

Workmen's tickets appeared for the first time in April 1885 with third class returns to:

	Workmen	Normal Fare
Idle	3d	4d
Eccleshill	3d	6d
Laisterdyke	3d	6d
St Dunstans	3d	6d
Bradford	3d	6d

There was also a blank ticket for other destinations. Workmen's tickets were available for outward journeys completed by 8am and for return after 12 noon though, in later years, return was permitted by any train the same day. They were the result of the Cheap Trains Act 1883 which laid down minimum facilities though some companies went beyond that especially after they began to experience tramway competition. The concept survived on British Railways until 1960 (see David R.

Smith's feature in *Railways Around Whitby, Volume Two*). The idea was almost the opposite of today's policy of charging higher fares in the morning peak.

It is difficult to measure the impact of workmen's fares at Shipley (GN). For May 1888 the number of tickets sold was 9,781 producing revenue of £132 18s 5d – not significantly different from May 1882. The numbers of workmen's returns issued in the month were:

Idle	78
Eccleshill	202
Laisterdyke	260
St Dunstans	7
Bradford	18
Stanningley	35
Manchester Road	34
Thornton	1
Dudley Hill	2
Morley	3
Blanks (i.e. others)	38

There is no compensating reduction in third class singles. Idle is up. Laisterdyke and Bradford are down.

One would really need to see ledgers for Idle and Eccleshill to get an idea of passenger usage of this branch.

Two 'Black Fives' start out from Idle in August 1958 with an excursion for Morecambe via the Calder Valley route.
(Peter Sunderland)

Tickets Issued at Shipley (GN) Station
May 1882

Destination	Class	Number	Fare s	Fare d	Revenue £	Revenue s	Revenue d
Bradford	1S	38½	5			16	0½
	2S	52	4			17	4
	3S	1,206	3		15	1	6
	3R	5	6			2	6
Laisterdyke	1S	8½	5			3	6½
	2S	17½	4			5	10
	3S	1,503½	3		18	15	10½
	3R	41½	6		1	0	9
Eccleshill	1S	6	5			2	6
	2S	14½	4			4	10
	3S	760½	3		9	10	1½
	3R	14	6			7	0
Idle	1S	19	4			6	4
	2S	30½	3			7	7½
	3S	2,531½	2		21	1	11
	1R	1½	8			1	0
	2R	1	6				6
	3R	31½	4			10	6
Thackley	1S	13	3			3	3
	2S	31	2			5	2
	3S	1,357	1½		8	10	10½
	1R	1	6				6
	3R	15½	3			3	10½
Stanningley	1S	2	8			1	4
	2S	4	6			2	0
	3S	193	5		4	0	5
	3R	2	10			1	8
Bramley	3S	64½	6		1	12	3
	1R	1½	1	6		2	3
Armley	3S	24	8			16	0
Holbeck	3S	5½	8½			3	11
Leeds	3S	43½	9		1	12	7½
Dudley Hill	3S	22½	5			9	4½
Birkenshaw	3S	11½	6			5	9
Drighlington	3S	16½	7			9	7½
Gildersome	3S	44	8		1	9	4
Morley	3S	34	9		1	5	6
Ardsley	3S	4½	10			3	9
Tingley	3S	14	10			11	8
Ossett	3S	7	1	1		7	7
Batley	3S	15½		10		12	11
Upper Batley	3S	3		9		2	3
Wakefield/ Westgate	2S	2	1	9		3	6
	3S	22	1	4	1	9	4
Pudsey/Greenside	3S	62		6½	1	13	7
Pudsey/Lowtown	3S	20		6		10	0
St Dunstans	1S	8		5		3	4
	2S	4½		4		1	6
	3S	414		3	5	3	6
Manchester Road	3S	39		3		9	9
Great Horton	3S	58		4		19	4
Clayton	1S	3		10		2	6
	3S	12		5½		5	6
Queensbury	3S	8		6½		4	4
Thornton	3S	12		8		8	0
Horton Park	3S	18½		4		6	2
Ovenden	3S	1		10			10
Dewsbury	3S	14		11		12	10
Holmfield	3S	1		9			9
North Bridge	3S	3		10½		2	7½
Halifax	3S	20½		10½		17	11½
Doncaster	3S	13	2	9½	1	16	4½
Tourist Tickets							
Skegness	3R	3	8	0	1	4	0
Mablethorpe	3R	2	8	0		16	0
Kings Cross	3R	10	10	0	5	0	0
York	3R	5	3	0		15	0
Doncaster	3R	2	3	6		7	0
Excursion Tickets							
Skegness	3R	173½	2	6	21	13	9
Boston	3R	12½	2	6	1	11	3
Nottingham	3R	4½	3	6		15	9
Foreign Tickets							
Halifax	3S	1		10½			10½
Grimsby	1R	1	6	0		6	0
Blank Tickets		24½			2	9	6
Excess Fares		49				9	4½
Monthly Totals		**9,239**			**£144**	**9**	**2½**

S=Single R= Return

N2 No 4736 passing St. Dunstans with a non stop Bradford to Leeds train, formed of GNR articulated bogie stock, on 15 September 1938.
(G.H. Butland)

The Methley Joint Railway

Fairburn 2-6-4T No 42073 (now preserved on the Lakeside & Haverthwaite Railway) calls at Ardsley with the 1.52pm (Saturdays Only) Castleford Central to Leeds Central on 5 November 1960.   *(D. Holmes)*

By an Act of 21 July 1863, the Bradford, Wakefield & Leeds Railway was authorised to change its name to the West Yorkshire Railway.   The same Act authorised a branch from a triangular junction north of Lofthouse to join both the North Eastern and Lancashire & Yorkshire Railways at Methley. Running powers were granted to the West Yorkshire Railway over the North Eastern to Castleford.

The North Eastern and Lancashire & Yorkshire didn't like this intrusion into their territory and the West Yorkshire could not afford to build the new line on its own. Therefore, by the Methley Railway Act 1864, it was arranged that the three companies should build the line at joint expense and that it should be administered by a joint committee to which each company would appoint two members.

The five-mile branch opened to goods in June 1865 but there was no regular passenger service until 1 May 1869 when the Great Northern Railway introduced one between Leeds Central and Castleford.

A service between Wakefield Westgate and Castleford began on 1 May 1876 by which time block signalling had been introduced on the Methley Joint and branch platforms had been provided at Lofthouse station. For a time this was known as Lofthouse Joint but from 1888 until closure in 1960 it was Lofthouse & Outwood.

At its east end, the Methley Joint crossed over the Midland Main Line (just north of Altofts & Whitwood station) then crossed over the Methley Junction to Castleford route of the North Eastern Railway.   It then came to Methley High Level Junction where it bifurcated passing through separate pairs of platforms in Methley Station. The south curve descended to join the North Eastern at Methley Joint Junction. The north curve joined the Lancashire & Yorkshire Railway at the confusingly named Lofthouse Junction. To the L&Y this was the junction for the line leading to Lofthouse.   At Lofthouse itself, there were three junctions called Lofthouse North, South and East effecting the connection with the Leeds to Wakefield line.

Methley Station, on the Joint Line was the third one to serve that township. Very close but at a lower level, was Methley Junction on the Lancashire & Yorkshire Railway.   The Midland Railway had a Methley Station over a mile to the north. British Railways tried to clarify the situation in the early 1950s by giving the suffix North to the Midland Station and South to that on the Joint Line. The L&Y Methley Junction had closed in 1943. North and

South then closed in 1957 and 1960 respectively.

The local passenger service over the Methley Joint was operated by the Great Northern Railway. In 1910 there were six trains per day, Mondays to Fridays from Leeds Central to Castleford and five from Wakefield Westgate to Castleford. The frequency was enhanced slightly on Saturdays but reduced on Sundays.

The final LNER timetable for Winter 1947/8 shows a better service from Leeds with ten departures Mondays to Fridays, eleven Saturdays but none on Sundays. From Wakefield Westgate there was just one to Castleford at 7am with no return working.

There were two other rail services between Leeds and Castleford. The North Eastern ran from Leeds New via Garforth to Castleford Central. That service ceased in 1951. The Lancashire & Yorkshire Railway went from Leeds Wellington to Castleford Cutsyke.

When diesel multiple units were introduced in 1957, the Methley Joint gained its best ever service with trains at almost hourly intervals between Leeds

Central and Castleford Central, most of them continuing to Pontefract Monkhill and Baghill. These lasted only until October 1964 when the Methley Joint closed to passengers.

There remained a handful of peak hour trains between Leeds City and Castleford Cutsyke – successors to the one time L&Y service. These were diverted to Castleford Central in 1968 and have since been increased to a half hourly frequency.

Observant travellers should be able to spot the abutments of the Methley Joint bridge and then the site of Methley Joint Junction as their train rounds the curve between Methley and Whitwood Junctions.

The Methley Joint closed to all traffic, west of the Newmarket Silkstone Colliery branch, in April 1965. The connection from Methley High Level Junction to the North Eastern closed in 1967 but, until February 1981, coal traffic kept open the section from the Colliery eastward to the L&Y connection at Lofthouse Junction (Methley).

These cloth capped gentlemen are hopefully going to exercise some care before crossing the track at Stanley. *(J.C.W. Halliday)*

Two J6 0-6-0s, 64222 and 64268 head a special through Stanley on 21 September 1958. The gas lamps have been modernised since the 1957 view on page ??.
(D. Butterfield/N.E. Stead Collection)

Methley South looking towards Leeds. The Castleford line is in the foreground. The other tracks lead to the junction with the Lancaster & Yorkshire Railway.
(Geoffrey Lewthwaite)

N1 No 69450 calls at Methley South with the 2.45pm Leeds Central to Castleford Central on 29 December 1956.
(D. Holmes)

V2 2-8-2 No 60977 passing Castleford Central in May 1959 with an express travelling towards York. The box and semaphore signals survived until 1997. One of the posters depicts Dixon of Dock Green advertising the Highway Code. *(Peter Sunderland)*

Locomotives On Shed

Two J39 0-6-0s 64796 and 64757 outside Ardsley Shed. To their right is No 68904, a 0-6-0T of Class J50 which were known as Ardsley tanks. The shed closed in October 1965.
(N.E. Stead Collection)

Copley Hill Shed stood within the triangle of lines between Holbeck, Wortley South and West Junctions. It was the Great Northern depot for Leeds and was home to main line passenger locos. A more humble ex GN Class J6 No 64277 is seen by the coaling stage. Copley Hill closed in September 1964.
(D. Butterfield/N.E. Stead Collection)

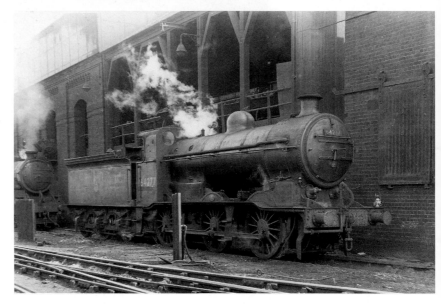

Hammerton Street (originally called Bowling) was the Great Northern shed for Bradford from 1876. N1 No 69443 is seen by the coaling stage in early BR days. After 1954, the shed was converted to maintain diesel multiple units and shunters. It closed in May 1984. *(N.E. Stead Collection)*

The 1882 Agreement

The Calder Viaduct on the Headfield Junction to Dewsbury Junction link during its first period of disuse in 1957.
(A.M. Ross)

The Spen Valley towns of Heckmondwike, Liversedge and Cleckheaton had been served by the Lancashire & Yorkshire Railway since 1849. There was a feeling, in the locality, that they would only get an adequate service to London if the Great Northern Railway were to reach them direct. Between 1871 and 1881, the GNR received written memorials and then actual deputations from the Spen Valley urging that an extension be built from Dewsbury.

Finally the GNR surveyed a route from just north of Dewsbury, through Heckmondwike, Liversedge, Cleckheaton and then on to Halifax. This would have paralleled the Lancashire & Yorkshire Railway virtually the whole way. In 1882 the GNR deposited a Bill in Parliament for the Dewsbury to Cleckheaton part of the scheme. In evidence before Parliament, the L&Y argued that considerable expense would be avoided if they and the GNR simply built a handful of short connecting lines between their two systems and arranged an exchange of running powers. This they agreed to do.

(1) The GN to build a short link from Hare Park, on the West Riding & Grimsby, to Crofton West Junction on the L&Y Knottingley to Wakefield line. This would give direct access from Doncaster to the Calder Valley route at Wakefield Kirkgate. The L&Y to have running powers over the GNR from Crofton to Doncaster.

(2) The GNR to rebuild the Pudsey branch so as to give a direct route from Leeds towards Dudley Hill and to build a line from Dudley Hill to Low Moor. The L&Y to have running powers from Leeds to Low Moor by this route.

(3) The GNR to build 1/2 mile link between Headfield Junction, on the L&Y Dewsbury Market Place branch, and Dewsbury Junction, south of Dewsbury Central. This would give access from Dewsbury Central to the L&Y Calder Valley and Spen Valley Lines.

(4) The L&Y to build a south curve at Low Moor giving direct access from Cleckheaton towards Halifax. The GNR to have running powers from Crofton West Junction to Halifax both via Brighouse and via Cleckheaton.

It took until 1893 for all these connections to be completed.

The Headfield Branch

The 1/2 mile branch was authorised by an Act of August 1883. Virtually the entire project was built on embankments or viaducts including one of 14 spans. Maximum gradient was 1 in 55 climbing towards Dewsbury. The double track opened for goods traffic in October 1887. No regular passenger train ran over it until December 1893.

Following withdrawal of the circular service in August 1914, the Headfield branch carried little traffic and was closed completely in May 1933. The embankment and viaducts remained in situ and the line was eventually re-laid as a single track, reopening for goods traffic on 15 February 1965. This coincided with closure of the route between Drighlington, Dewsbury Central and Wakefield. It enabled a link to be maintained from Dewsbury GN goods depot direct to the Marshalling Yard at Healey Mills, on the ex L&Y Calder Valley Main Line.

Dewsbury goods depot closed in 1989, since when the Headfield branch has stood derelict again.

The Pudsey Loop

N1 0-6-2T No 69483 entering Pudsey Lowtown with the 12.25 Leeds Central to Bradford Exchange on 30 January 1954. *(M. Goodall)*

The Leeds, Bradford & Halifax Junction Railway had missed Pudsey so as to avoid even steeper gradients. The town centre stands just over 1/2 mile from Stanningley station but at a higher level.

A branch line was authorised by the GNR Act of 24 July 1871 to commence at both Stanningley and Bramley. A contract was awarded for construction of the line in February 1875. The formation was built for double track. There were three underbridges and seven overbridges in the 1 3/4 miles from Stanningley to Pudsey Greenside. In the interest of economy only a single track was built initially, whilst no track at all was laid on the branch from Bramley.

Goods traffic began during the summer of 1877. A passenger service of 15 trains each way, weekdays only, began on 1 April 1878, starting from a bay platform at Stanningley. The intermediate station at Pudsey Lowtown was on a 1 in 50 gradient and the Government Inspector would not sanction its opening on a single line. Trains began to stop at Lowtown from 1 July 1878 by which time it had been equipped with a second platform, loop line and catch point.

The branch was worked by staff and ticket until it was doubled later on.

Extension of the Pudsey branch came as a result of the 1882 accord between the GNR and the Lancashire & Yorkshire Railway. Due to financial constraints, it was not until 1893 that work was completed. The extension took two forms. First the

A class 110 'Calder Valley' dmu pulls away from Pudsey Greenside bound for Bradford in May 1964. The main buildings are at a strange angle because they follow the original terminal alignment. A rake of excursion coaches is stabled in the yard.
(Peter Sunderland)

branch was transformed into a loop off the main Leeds to Bradford line. In addition it was connected to the Dudley Hill to Low Moor line dealt with in the next chapter.

Track was laid from Bramley but no junction was created where it met the existing line from Stanningley as this was disconnected at the Pudsey end and used as a siding. From Pudsey Greenside, the line was extended through a 618 yard tunnel then along a very high embankment to join the Ardsley to Laisterdyke line at Cutlers Junction.

In 1910 there were some 24 trains each way on the Pudsey Loop but the service was anything but regular. Some trains were through from Leeds Central to Bradford Exchange, others from Leeds Central to Pudsey Greenside and some from Bramley to Bradford Exchange. At times it was necessary to change at Bramley to get from Leeds to Pudsey.

There had, since 4 June 1908, been an electric tram service from Leeds to Pudsey, less comfortable than the trains and slower but much more frequent and to a more central terminus in Pudsey. The GNR did nothing whatever to respond to this competition.

The 1922 timetable still shows the effect of wartime cuts. There were 14 scheduled passenger trains each weekday eastbound, and 17 westbound, the majority being through from Leeds Central to Bradford Exchange. There was no service round the Pudsey loop on a Sunday.

The summer 1938 service was only marginally better, still with no Sunday trains.

From 14 June 1954, the branch was served by Derby Lightweight diesel multiple units. Unlike the basic half hourly service via Stanningley, the Pudsey branch trains were not at regular intervals. The average frequency was about hourly but slightly erratic. All were through from Leeds Central to Bradford Exchange usually calling also at Armley Moor, Bramley and Laisterdyke which were missed by nearly all the direct trains via Stanningley.

The Pudsey Loop was an early casualty of the Beeching Report. At the TUCC hearing BR claimed that traffic had risen with the diesels but had then fallen back. From 1961 some off peak trains were withdrawn. By 1963 there were about 220 passengers a day in total at the two Pudsey stations. They closed on 13 June 1964. Three weeks later the branch closed completely. Armley Moor, Bramley and Laisterdyke were then served by a handful of trains via Stanningley until they succumbed on 2 July 1966. Stanningley itself closed on 30 December 1967 but only after a new station had been built to serve the Pudsey area.

B1 4-6-0 No 61034 'Chiru' and 'Black Five' No 44695 pause at Pudsey Greenside with an excursion from Bradford to Cleethorpes on 30 May 1964.
(D. Holmes)

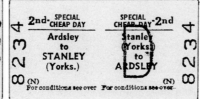

Pudsey – Dudley Hill – Low Moor

A principal objective of the 1882 agreement with the Lancashire & Yorkshire Railway had been to achieve a more direct route from Leeds to the Spen Valley towns of Cleckheaton, Liversedge and Heckmondwike.

This was done by means of a curve from Tyersal Junction, 1½ miles west of Pudsey Greenside, to Broad Lane Junction, ¾ mile north of Dudley Hill. Between Broad Lane and Dudley Hill, the track was quadrupled so traffic from Pudsey direction could continue independently through separate platforms at Dudley Hill then dive under the Drighlington line in order to reach Low Moor. Here there was a junction with the Lancashire & Yorkshire Railway, just north of the station. There was also a separate GNR goods depot.

From 1 December 1893, a circular passenger service was introduced jointly by the GNR and Lancashire & Yorkshire Railways. Trains travelled from Leeds Central via Bramley, Pudsey Lowtown and Greenside, Dudley Hill, Low Moor, the Spen Valley, Thornhill, Dewsbury Central, Batley, Tingley and Beeston in order to regain Leeds Central 1 1/2 hours and 30 miles later. The service began with seven trains one way round and six the other. The 13 trains were worked 9 by the GNR and 4 by the L&YR which more or less reflected their respective shares of the route mileage.

This gave the three Spen Valley towns their direct service to Leeds but it was eclipsed in 1900 when the London & North Western Railway opened its 'Leeds New Line'. This offered a much shorter route from the three towns into Leeds albeit that the LNWR station at Cleckheaton was inconveniently sited. By 1910 the circular service was down to three trains each way, two on Sundays. This represented the entire passenger service over the Dudley Hill to Low Moor line. Other parts of the route saw a variety of other trains.

The circular service was withdrawn at the end of August 1914. The Dudley Hill to Low Moor section then fell into virtual disuse and was closed in 1917 so that the track could be lifted for use elsewhere.

The Tyersal to Broad Lane curve fared a little better, finally closing about 1952. The last train to use it was an afternoon goods from Wakefield to Leeds via Gildersome, Dudley Hill and Pudsey.

For many years the curve had retained a solitary passenger train in one direction only. In 1910, there had been two unbalanced workings. The 7.04am from Dewsbury Central called at Batley, Drighlington, Dudley Hill and then all stations to Leeds Central via Pudsey. The 1.11pm from Ossett followed the same route calling at all stations except Upper Batley or Drighlington. By 1922, the morning train had gone but the afternoon one was still running at 1.15pm from Ossett, now missing only Drighlington. It is still shown in 1938, starting from Wakefield Westgate at 12.55pm, calling at every station to Leeds Central via Dewsbury and Pudsey.

Low Moor goods depot closed in May 1933 but the shed was retained in non railway use. It can still be seen from Bradford to Halifax trains as they speed past the ill-fated 'Transperience' complex.

2-6-4T No 42141 climbs the 1 in 50 towards Dudley Hill with the Saturdays only 8.52 Bradford to Cleethorpes on 8 August 1964. The loop in the foreground was one part of the pair of tracks leading from Pudsey to Low Moor. *(M. Mitchell)*

Batley to Beeston

Tingley Viaduct carried the Batley to Beeston branch over the Leeds to Wakefield main line. A class V2 2-6-2 is in charge of a London express.
(A.M. Ross)

A landmark on the line between Wakefield and Leeds is the tall five arch viaduct under which trains pass shortly after emerging from Ardsley Tunnel. There hasn't been anything on top of this structure since 1953. It stands as a monument to yet another Great Northern branch, built at no small expense to compete with an earlier railway already providing a direct link, in this case, from Leeds to Batley and Dewsbury.

As today's express speeds towards Leeds, one can look up to the right and see the disused formation curving off the viaduct and sweeping down to join the main line more than a mile to the north at what was Beeston Junction. Look even more closely before reaching Beeston Junction and you can see the abutments of a bridge which used to carry the Leeds bound track back across the main line so as to join it on the left hand side.

The Batley to Beeston route was authorised in 1881 but no work was undertaken until the Summer of 1887 apart from the relatively easy first half mile

between Batley West Junction and Soothill Wood Colliery. This section opened to coal traffic in the Autumn of 1887.

The flying junction at Beeston was not part of the original scheme but was authorised later by an Act of July 1889.

The route was in two parts: From Batley West Junction to Tingley West and from Tingley East to Beeston Junction. Earthworks were heavy with deep cuttings, high embankments, ten underbridges, the five arch, 62 feet high viaduct over the main line and the 659 yard tunnel at Soothill. There was an intermediate station at Woodkirk. Tingley Station was rebuilt on the same site in anticipation of the new route opening.

Goods traffic began on 1 July 1890. Two quarries were sited to the north west of Woodkirk. These gained a rail connection in 1892. There was a maximum gradient of 1 in 33 on the internal quarry system.

The passenger service commenced on 1 August

1890 with six trains each way between Leeds Central and Dewsbury Central. From November 1890 some trains ran in a circle from Leeds via Batley, Dewsbury, Ossett and back to Leeds via Wrenthorpe and Ardsley. L&Y trains ran from Leeds Central to Barnsley Exchange via Beeston, Batley and Dewsbury Central, then via Headfield Junction to reach Horbury & Ossett.

From 1 December 1893, the Batley to Beeston route was used by the joint GN/L&Y service mentioned in the previous chapter which made a circuit from Leeds Central via Pudsey, the Spen Valley, Dewsbury and back to Leeds.

Looking at the 1910 timetable, the GNR offered up to 17 weekday trains between Leeds Central Batley and Dewsbury. What was so complicated was where they went after Dewsbury.

The 6.32am from Leeds arrived Dewsbury at 6.58. After a quick turn round it left at 7.04 for Leeds Central via Drighlington and Pudsey. The 8.45am from Leeds appears to have no return working from Dewsbury.

By 1938, the service was reduced. Gone was the circular route via Cleckheaton, the Barnsley trains and the Sunday service. Mondays to Fridays, there were ten departures from Leeds to Dewsbury, most going on to Wakefield Westgate or coming back to Leeds via Ossett and Wrenthorpe.

Woodkirk station closed on 23 September 1939. The LNER timetable for Winter 1947/8 shows just six trains from Leeds Central, all through to Wakefield

	Departures from Leeds Central	Ultimate Destination
	5.15 am	Wakefield Westgate
	6.32	Dewsbury Central
	8.45	Dewsbury Central
	8.55	Barnsley
	9.09	Leeds Central via Ossett
	10.45	Leeds Central via Cleckheaton
	11.55	Leeds Central via Ossett
	12.20 pm	Ossett
	2.13	Barnsley
	2.35	Wakefield Westgate
	4.15	Leeds Central via Cleckheaton
	5.40	Leeds Central via Cleckheaton
	6.35	Ossett
	7.00	Barnsley
	8.25	Leeds Central via Ossett
TuThSO	9.35	Ardsley via Ossett
TuSX	10.30	Leeds Central via Ossett
TuThSO	10.58	Ossett
SUNDAYS		
	8.25 am	Leeds Central via Cleckheaton
	12.05 pm	Dewsbury Central
	4.25	Leeds Central via Cleckheaton
	8.35	Ossett

Westgate. There is an extra on Saturdays but only five trains the other way and nothing on Sundays.

The remaining passenger service over the Batley to Beeston line was withdrawn in October 1951. The line closed completely in July 1953 except between Woodkirk and Tingley. This section remained open until 1964 to serve the quarries at Woodkirk.

Woodkirk Station looking towards Tingley in August 1961.   (M. Mitchell)

Industrial Locomotives

When steam finished on British Railways in 1968, a number of enthusiasts found solace on colliery and other industrial lines where some quite ancient locomotives were still working.

With the subsequent decline of heavy industry, it is not just the engines but most of the industrial sites themselves which have become memories.

'St. Johns', seen at East Ardsley Colliery on 4 July 1964, was a 0-4-0 Peckett dating from 1922. The Colliery was served by a main line connection on the south west side between Ardsley loco shed and station.

(Martin Bairstow Collection)

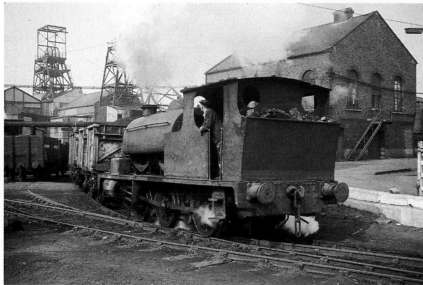

Roundwood Colliery was reached by a short branch running to the south east between Alverthorpe and Flushdyke. Hudswell Clarke 0-6-0ST No 23 is seen in action at the Colliery on 12 May 1962.

(John Holroyd)

Cohens Foundry had a private siding at Stanningley on the north side of the main line. It made a level crossing with the Pudsey branch of Leeds City Tramways. Hunslet 0-6-0ST No 600 was photographed in 1964.

(Martin Bairstow Collection)

The Diamond Jubilee

Bob Watson has also loaned a copy of the GNR Working Timetable and Special Working Notices for the week ending Saturday 26 June 1897. The publication runs to 87 pages numbered 814 to 900. Assuming they started at page 1 in January, then this edition is extra large because of Queen Victoria's Diamond Jubilee which fell on Tuesday 22 June.

The book is a mine of information beginning with routine announcements including lists of lost season tickets and missing milk churns. It gives specimens of certificates to be presented as proof of entitlement to reduced fares by members of such worthy organisations as the National Temperance Choral Union, the Tonic Sol-Fa Association and the Mid-Herts Golf Club.

A lot of information concerns details of ordinary timetabled trains by which excursion tickets may be issued. Every Saturday, for example, customers from a handful of West Riding stations may book one, three, four or six day excursion tickets to various stations south of Doncaster. Departure from Bradford Exchange is at 6.50am but the connection from Keighley leaves at 4.58am giving a lengthy wait in Bradford. Return is also by specified trains at rather more sociable hours.

On Tuesdays and Saturdays during June, half day excursion tickets are issued by two specified ordinary trains between stations Bradford Exchange to Great Horton and stations Denholme to Ingrow. A similar facility is available Thursdays and Saturdays from stations in the Halifax area and on Wednesdays and Saturdays from stations Leeds Central to Stanningley, again to Denholme, Wilsden, Cullingworth and Ingrow.

A hundred years ago, just as today, if you wanted the cheapest fare, you may have had to put yourself out. If you wanted complete flexibility then you had to pay a higher price.

A special train for the 'Volunteers' left Bradford Exchange for Kings Cross at 3.30pm on Monday 21 June, comprising one composite, one first class saloon (no doubt for the officers), one third class saloon, three 5 compartment thirds and a brake third at each end. It stopped at St Dunstans, for the connection from Halifax, and ran via Leeds Central stopping at Holbeck inward only to pick up the 'Ripon contingent'.

The miners were celebrating the Jubilee on the Monday with eight special trains from the GNR alone converging on Barnsley between 9.19 and 11.23am. One was from Chickenley Heath and intermediate stations to Wakefield Westgate for the Ossett and Roundwood miners. Another was from Laisterdyke and all stations via Tingley to Wakefield Westgate. The Manchester, Sheffield & Lincolnshire Railway was to provide pilot drivers and guards from Wakefield to Barnsley Court House. Together with ordinary trains and other companies' specials, these workings must have imposed severe pressure on Barnsley. Drivers, firemen and guards were instructed 'not to leave their respective trains at

Barnsley until they have been placed in readiness for the return journey. They must be on duty at their respective trains at least one hour before they are timed to leave Barnsley' (in the evening).

Practically every GN station in the West Riding offered the opportunity of a one, two, four or five day excursion to London leaving at about midnight on Monday 21st. One train left Holmfield at the stroke of midnight running via North Bridge, Halifax, the Calder Valley, and Wakefield Kirkgate whence it would have to be propelled up to Westgate to join the portion from Leeds Central. This had left at 12.38am calling at Holbeck (connection from Stanningley) and Ardsley (connection from Castleford). The combined train of 15 third class carriages then called at Sandal, Nostell, Doncaster and plenty of other places before reaching Kings Cross at 6.04am.

The second train left Keighley at midnight calling at all stations to Manchester Road then non stop to Howden Clough, Batley, Dewsbury Central, Ossett and Wakefield Westgate where it was joined by the portion which had left Bradford Exchange at 12.23am. This had called at Laisterdyke (connection from Shipley, Idle and Eccleshill), all stations to Morley then Wakefield Westgate. The combined train of 14 carriages then served Hemsworth and South Elmsall on its way to Kings Cross which was reached at 6.18am Tuesday morning. Passengers going only for the one day of the Jubilee returned from Kings Cross at 2.40am Wednesday reaching the West Riding around 8.00am.

The Jubilee day was a public holiday with nationwide celebrations. Some used the opportunity for a day out. Messrs Hollingrake & Clegg reserved three 9 coach special trains which left Pellon at 5.40, 5.55 and 6.07am for Morecambe via Queensbury and Keighley where Midland locomotives took over. Arrival back in Pellon was at 9.50, 10.00 and 10.10pm. A first class coach was to be provided on one of the trains, labelled and reserved for the Committee.

There was no holiday for the signalmen at Pellon where both No. 1 and No. 2 boxes had to be open from 4.50am 'until the last empty coach special has left and is out of section. Mr Ingle to arrange'. In the morning, the three empty trains came from Laisterdyke to which they returned after discharging their passengers at Pellon in the evening.

The Halifax Clarion Vocal Union chartered a ten coach special leaving Halifax at 7.30am, picking up at North Bridge and Ovenden before finding its way to Bolton Abbey. Again the train came from Laisterdyke, charged with gas, and was worked by the Midland from Keighley via Skipton.

A half day public excursion ran from Keighley (depart 1.10pm) to Manchester Victoria calling at most stations to Halifax. It was worked by an L&Y loco and carriages which had first to be run empty to Keighley. The return was at 11.15pm from Manchester Victoria arriving Keighley at 1.06 the

69464 waits departure for Bradford via Queensbury at Halifax in 1955. Another N1 (on the left) with a Keighley train. This part of Halifax Station is now the Eureka Children's Museum. *(Peter Sunderland)*

following morning. A Great Northern pilot driver and guard were required between Holmfield and Keighley.

A public day excursion ran from Bradford, via Dewsbury, and from Leeds to Skegness, the two portions joining at Wakefield Westgate.

There must have been a major event at Worksop to which a special left Halifax at 7.12am running via Queensbury, Bradford Exchange and Dewsbury, then joining with the Leeds portion at Wakefield Westgate. Connections were advertised by ordinary train from Keighley, St Pauls, Shipley, Stanningley, Pudsey and most intermediate stations. The Halifax portion comprised seven vehicles including a third class saloon labelled and reserved for the Halifax Thursday Cycling Club. The Leeds portion was to be five third class. A second engine was required between Halifax and Bradford both ways. The High Level branch train was required to do an extra trip at 10.28pm from Holmfield to St Pauls in connection with the return excursion. All other connections were by ordinary train.

For those who didn't have to return to work on Wednesday, there was 'a half day trip with three or four day bookings' to Cleethorpes from Bradford Exchange (1.13pm) and Leeds Central (1.35pm). It was intended to join the trains at Wakefield Westgate but the loco department was 'to be prepared' to run the two trains independently all the way to Cleethorpes, if necessary.

On Saturday 26 June there were day and half day excursions from Halifax to Morecambe changing at Keighley. This facility utilised Midland Railway special trains from Keighley but it was necessary to increase ordinary train lengths between Halifax and Keighley. This arrangement had also been used on the Jubilee Tuesday for public excursions to Morecambe.

As Saturday 26 June was Halifax Summer Fair, a number of other carriage working diagrams were to be increased to 7 or 8 coaches.

There were day trips to York, Castle Howard and Scarborough from many West Riding stations. One train began from Keighley (via Pudsey) and from Batley amalgamating at Stanley. The other originated from Halifax (via Holmfield and Morley) and from Bradford (via Stanningley) again joining at Stanley and proceeding via Castleford just behind the first excursion. Journey time from Keighley to Scarborough was about four hours. You got ten hours at the seaside and a very late return home, the signal boxes having to remain open until the empty stock was finally out of section.

It is hoped that the foregoing is of some interest as social as much as railway history. Very few people had ever seen Queen Victoria but all had been taught to respect her. In an age when breaks from daily routine were very rare, the Jubilee must have been very welcome.

My older colleagues at work will remember the name Hollingrake & Clegg. A hundred years ago they could fill three trains from Pellon to Morecambe. Thirty years ago, our firm was involved in their liquidation.

79

0-4-4T, No 682, seen at Leeds Central, was one of 16 'West Riding Tanks' built at Doncaster between 1881 and 1885.
(Martin Bairstow Collection)

Pellon Station looking towards St. Pauls in 1929. At that time the line was still signalled. The passenger station was closed to normal traffic but still used occasionally for excursions. *(Tom Chapman)*

Excursion traffic remained popular until the Beeching period. 42073 and 61115 double head a Leeds to Blackpool working which called at Pudsey Greenside on 30 May 1964, a fortnight before closure. *(D. Holmes)*

Relief Station Master

In 1993 I was privileged to meet retired Station Master Frank Kipling at his home at Thornhill. He was then aged 86. He died in 1994.

Frank George Kipling joined the Great Northern Railway shortly before his sixteenth birthday in 1922. His first appointment was as a lad messenger at City Road Goods Depot, Bradford.

He quickly trained as a booking clerk and moved to Great Horton Station in 1923 thus beginning the long progression up the clerk's scale which gave annual increments to the age of 31.

The neighbouring station at Horton Park did not employ a clerk, just porters under a station master. The Horton Park Station Master spent a lot of time in a sweet shop at the other side of Horton Park Avenue. One day he eloped with the lady from the sweet shop possibly absconding with both the station and shop takings. The LNER cut its losses (or possibly began to recover them) by abolishing the post of station master at Horton Park and placing it under Great Horton.

Frank Kipling was sent to cover the booking office at Horton Park. He reorganised the ticket rack, moving it nearer to the window. Then they sent Charlie Cook, a trainee clerk straight from school, who was too small to reach the rack in its new position so Frank made some steps for him out of old drawers.

There was a milk traffic from Cullingworth and Wilsden to Great Horton and Horton Park. The empties returned from Horton Park at 3.28 in the afternoon. This departure was often witnessed by children from local 'posh houses' with their nursemaids.

Once Charlie Cook was trained, Frank moved back to Great Horton. In 1926, he was living in a cottage near Duckett's crossing, between Hillfoot Tunnel and Laisterdyke. In order to get to work, he walked along the track to Laisterdyke Station where he caught a train changing at St Dunstans. One morning he encountered a headless corpse on the track which he duly reported on arrival at Laisterdyke. Nobody there was interested as their responsibility ended at the bridge carrying the Shipley branch - 'try Pudsey', they said.

Pudsey claimed that the body lay within the jurisdiction of Stanningley Station. Stanningley tried to throw responsibility back on to Pudsey but was eventually persuaded to send staff to deal with it.

Frank decided that it might be easier in future to take the slightly longer route by road but one morning he stumbled upon the body of a man who had shot himself near Thornbury Cricket Field. After that he tried walking the other way by footpath through Tyersal, south of the railway line. But accidents come in threes, as Frank discovered when he found police fishing a body out of a quarry alongside his new walking route.

From Great Horton, Frank transferred to Dudley Hill Goods Yard which was particularly busy at this time with materials arriving for the building of the housing estate at Holmwood. Cement came from Ellesmere Port, slates from Blaenau Ffestiniog and window frames from Nottinghamshire.

After a spell on both goods and passenger work at Dudley Hill, Frank Kipling moved on to Laisterdyke where he was to remain for most of the 1930s.

He did have a period lodging at South Elmsall where he was also in charge of Hampole Station which despatched a lot of peas.

Whilst sitting in the booking office at Laisterdyke, Frank received a telephone call from one of the signal boxes instructing him to call an ambulance because the train recording lad had got a signal lever up his (posterior). After some protest, Frank was prevailed upon to carry out the instruction and

The northbound 'Yorkshire Pullman' passing Ardsley on 28 June 1961 behind Class A3 No 60039 'Sandwich'.
(D. Holmes)

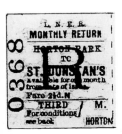

81

in due course the lad was carried down the signalbox steps. Apparently there had been three levers pulled over. The lad had attempted to leap frog over the middle one using the two outer ones for support. He lost his grip with dire consequences. The damage was not permanent. During the subsequent Second World War, the lad rose to the rank of lieutenant commander in the Royal Navy. When he was demobbed afterwards, the LNER offered him his job back as a porter but he was not satisfied with that and failed to take up the invitation.

Frank was still booking tickets at Laisterdyke at the start of the Second World War. An enemy aircraft hit a wagon of butter in Quarry Gap sidings with an incendiary bomb setting the place alight and making it a target for further attack. Staff in the yard tried to get an engine to shunt the blazing wagon under the water column but they were attacked with machine gun fire. They all took refuge under Dick Lane bridge apart from Yard Inspector Harry England who was deaf and oblivious to the danger.

Cutlers Junction signalbox lost its toilet in the raid. Shrapnel passed through Laisterdyke East box where Joseph Kipling, Frank's father was on duty.

At West Box, which stood on a gantry, the steps were blown off leaving signalman Cyril Wattam marooned. When the Box was hit again, he had to shin down an adjacent telegraph pole with injury to his hands.

Frank himself was not far from danger as a bomb exploded outside the booking office. The ticket rack was destroyed. Tickets ended up everywhere including along the up platform and Frank spent the next day, Sunday gathering them up and sorting them out.

Rails were twisted and traffic was interrupted over the remainder of the weekend but trains were running again on Monday, a platelayer's cabin deputising for the damaged West Box.

The roof over the staircase onto the down platform had been blown off and was never restored.

In 1942, Frank Kipling was appointed a relief station master nominally based at Ardsley though he continued to live in Bradford. The LNER had other relief station masters based at Leeds, Bradford and Wakefield. Between them they covered for annual leave, sickness and any other vacancies at all LNER stations in the West Riding.

Sometimes the appointment might be for an odd day, sometimes a week, occasionally a fortnight. At that time station masters worked six days per week with a half day alternately mid week and on Saturdays. Inevitably, when planning a holiday, the regular man preferred to finish work on Saturday dinner time then have off the week which would have involved working Saturday afternoon. The relief man invariably got the worse deal.

Frank still has his note book recording all the stations he visited. The relief man could sometimes fall into a trap which the regular incumbent would have known to avoid. At Denholme, during the War, he was alerted by lady porter Amy to what she considered was a major embankment fire. It was all hands to the stirrup pump. This piece of machinery was not functioning too well and they got water everywhere. Amy had to adjourn to put her coat on but eventually they got the fire out. Then a platelayer appeared pleading that he had used two boxes of matches getting the fire going. He was trying to burn the vegetation by day because there had been problems with locomotives starting fires during the blackout.

A relief station master would expect to find things in reasonable order when he arrived at a station. On one of his very few visits to Ingrow, a Monday probably in August 1945, Frank found half the staff missing. By that time the LNER station master also had charge of the adjacent LMS station on the Worth Valley branch. On this occasion, the LMS clerk was on holiday, the porter was sick and

Joseph W. Kipling, Frank's father, was a signalman at Laisterdyke East from 1909 until 1941.

(Frank Kipling Collection)

the station was being run by the LNER goods checker, an obliging chap who seemed to be enjoying himself booking passengers instead of his usual job.

The LNER porter signalman was also missing so Frank had to arrange for the two signalmen to go onto overtime so as to cover for the short middle turn which was normally done by the porter signalman. This man's other duties included cleaning the carriages which were stabled at Ingrow so Frank swept them out himself.

Nobody had thought to leave behind the key to the safe in the LMS booking office so Frank was unable to get at the previous day's takings. He was supposed to send these in a sealed leather bag to Keighley. Some time later, Frank received a demand from the internal audit department to explain why he had not forwarded Sunday's takings.

In March 1946, a request was received from the LNER at Cambridge for six relief station masters. The Leeds Area responded with the offer that they could spare just one - Frank Kipling - who was to spend two weeks at Wimblington, a place he had never heard of previously which was located just south of March on the line to St. Ives.

Arriving mid afternoon on the Monday, Frank sought digs and was lucky to bump into a chap who was able to fix him up at a local pub. His good fortune continued when he sat down to evening meal to find that food rationing had, apparently, failed to catch on in this part of the world. They went short of nothing.

The only commodity which was in limited supply was railway wagons for which every station seemed desperate. During Frank's stay, a train of empties left Whitemoor Yard, March, for Cambridge with 76 on but arrived just engine and brake after each intermediate station had succeeded in getting half a dozen into their yard.

The wagons were needed for loading straw and other farm produce. This needed bags which could be hired from the railway company subject to a complicated price structure with which the station master had to be familiar.

A relief station master could never win. If he was too conversant with local conditions, he was taunted as a 'know all'. If he had no idea then he was a 'know nowt'. Frank preferred the latter endearment so he concealed his previous experience with sacks and allowed his local staff the pleasure of imparting their knowledge upon him.

Frank's first permanent station was Stanley on the Methley Joint to which he moved in July 1948. His bedroom was above the down waiting room. The first train, at 5.20 in the morning, used to convey miners to Methley. On Monday mornings they would wake Mr and Mrs Kipling as they enthused noisily about Saturday's match at Wakefield Trinity. Frank would bang on the bedroom floor with his boot, and the porter would warn them that 't'boss would be after them'. When they returned in the early afternoon, they would apologise blaming the shortest one of their number for the disturbance.

Frank's job was to sell rail travel so he would visit the local Working Men's Club or Miners' Welfare to enquire about arrangements for the annual outing. Frank knew his customers' requirements and could offer a BG in the middle of the train where they could set up a bar. He would assure them that, whilst travelling by train to the seaside, it would be as if the Club had never closed. Then he could offer free first class returns to the Committee allowing them a preview trip to ensure satisfactory arrangements at the other end.

The station master at Stanley also had charge of Methley South as well as the sidings at New Market Colliery which was located between the two.

During the period January to March each year, Stanley despatched up to seven or eight wagons of rhubarb each day. An engine came from Ardsley with a brake van to pick up the loaded wagons which were taken to Doncaster. There they were shunted on to the front of the Aberdeen to London fish and meat train for delivery to Covent Garden next morning.

On Summer Saturdays, holiday and excursion trains used to amalgamate at Stanley. A portion would arrive (say) from Bradford via Dewsbury. The loco would propel the carriages back over the cross onto the up line then abandon them. The portion from Leeds would then arrive, propel back onto the other coaches, then continue with the full train bound for Bridlington or other holiday destinations. The station master had to make sure that the catch points were clamped on the up line west of the station. In the other direction, the operation was easier. The Leeds train would simply leave the Bradford carriages in Stanley platform until an engine came to rescue them. It is always a more simple operation to divide a loco hauled train than it is to amalgamate one.

Freight also used to divide at Stanley so that different portions could take the Ardsley and Lofthouse curves when they reached the end of the Methley Joint. On one occasion, a double headed freight arrived at 2am westbound (up direction). It proceeded to reverse over onto the down main to leave the rear portion in Stanley platform. The wagons would wait here until an engine came to take them forward. In the meantime they would block the down line but it was the middle of the night with no passenger traffic wanting to pass.

Unfortunately the two locos set off for Ardsley with their remaining half load so fast that they broke the coupling between the rear engine and the leading wagon. The train rolled back and was diverted by trap points into the yard, demolishing a gas lamp as it went. The rear of the train ended up the embankment.

Frank's first job was to find the stop tap for the gas lamp before he could contemplate allowing a steam locomotive near the scene especially as the train included paraffin tanks. There was a tow rope in the guards van which they attached to the engines and so removed the front vehicle which was loaded

'Black Five' 4-6-0 No 44951 passing Laisterdyke with an excursion heading towards Leeds at Whitsun 1966.
(D.J. Mitchell)

An ex North Eastern Railway G5 No 67311 pulls into Stanley with a Leeds Central to Castleford Central train in February 1957.
(P.B. Booth/N.E. Stead Collection)

with ten tons of flour. They got this and the other wagons which were still on the track over onto the down side and into a siding. The 5.20 down passenger train was able to pass but they had to work to clear the up line for when it returned.

Only after the morning rush hour had passed did they get the breakdown train to tackle the vehicles which were off the road.

Promotion came in 1952 with a move to Ovenden with responsibility also for North Bridge and Holmfield. The previous station master at Ovenden had volunteered to take on Holmfield also in return for an upward regrading when the man there was transferred to Greetland. He still lived in the Holmfield Station House. Frank moved into the detached residence alongside Ovenden Station.

There was a clerk and two porters at Ovenden but with no goods facilities, no signal box, just two plain tracks there should be little scope for crises or emergencies. Most mornings Frank caught the 8.30 train to Holmfield where all his correspondence was delivered.

One morning he was still having a shave at about 8 o'clock when the porter summoned him to have a look at a passenger who appeared to be unwell. Actually the man was dead but as Frank paused to think what to do next, he chanced to notice a policeman walking across the road bridge. So he fetched him. The officer enquired whether Frank knew the man's name – no but he thought he knew where he lived. Did he have a wife? Frank believed he did but said he didn't fancy breaking the news to her. The policeman reassured Frank that he was used to this type of situation and that the matter could be left in his capable hands.

Some days later the two met again and Frank asked the policeman how he had got on. No problem. First he had called on a neighbour to solicit her assistance. Then the two of them had presented themselves at the door of the newly bereaved who opened the conversation:

Is it about George? (or whatever her husband's name was)

– It would seem so.

Has he had an accident?

– It would seem so.

Is he dead?

– It would seem so.

There was no GPO telephone at Ovenden but Frank did have internal phones at the bottom of his bedroom steps allowing either Leeds or Manchester controls to call him out in an emergency. When a driver reported a possible obstruction in Queensbury Tunnel, Frank had to walk the line all the way to Queensbury during the night but he found nothing.

A genuine emergency arose when blasting for an extension to Crossley's Mill at Dean Clough caused damage to the viaduct and the engineer declared the up (Bradford bound) line unfit for use. Frank instituted single line working over the down line acting as pilot man himself. It was Saturday and

when he asked for relief nobody was forthcoming so he had to keep going until the last train had passed through.

The emergency single line section was between North Bridge North Box and Holmfield. Normal double track block still operated between North Bridge North and Halifax East. North Bridge South Box had switched out and closed.

When the last train had gone, the North Bridge North signalman gave the box closing signal to Halifax East. The man there refused to accept it saying that you could not close a box with single line working still in force. The North Bridge man appealed to Frank who agreed that this was nonsense for two reasons. First, the single line section was in the other direction, not towards Halifax. Second, once the last train had gone, they weren't operating any type of working. They wanted to go home rather than spend all night arguing so Frank said 'give him six bells (meaning obstruction danger) he can't refuse that.'

Halifax East duly accepted 'obstruction danger' and was then obliged to carry out the emergency procedure placing detonators on the viaduct leading towards North Bridge to protect the 'obstruction'.

There were no trains on Sunday. On Monday morning North Bridge South Box opened as usual and accepted the first train from Halifax East. This exploded the detonators and came to a halt. Reports were called for.

Saturday 21 May 1955 saw the end of regular passenger service at North Bridge, Ovenden and Holmfield affording Frank a modicum of newspaper publicity. He was quoted in the *Halifax Courier* as having experienced an upsurge in ticket sales during the final week not because more people were travelling but because many of the tickets still bore the legend 'Halifax & Ovenden Joint Railway'. One man apparently 'paid for tickets from Ovenden to various stations on the line'. (Our friend and ardent ticket connoisseur, Geoffrey Lewthwaite denies that it was him).

On the actual day of closure, the newspaper carried a brief biography of the 'Three – Stations Master' as they called him. Frank says now that he did not regard the passenger closure as marking the beginning of the end of the line because 'there was still plenty of freight'. This contemporary view is confirmed by John Oxley who spoke to Frank and other staff in May 1955. There probably was a feeling that the remaining railway operation would go on for ever. After all the adjacent Halifax High Level Line had already survived for nearly 40 years since the withdrawal of passenger service.

The High Level branch now came under the jurisdiction of the Ovenden Station Master who also took over the work of the North Bridge goods agent. There was still a fair amount of traffic. Holmfield still employed a goods foreman, a checker, two goods porters and a shunter. Pellon managed just one shunter who also covered St Pauls as required. Holmfield Box was still manned on two shifts.

69464 brings its Bradford to Halifax train to a stand at Ovenden on 14 May 1955. Station Master Kipling hopes for some custom. *(J.C.W Halliday)*

J50 0-6-0T No 68923 climbs through Ovenden with a mixed freight on 14 May 1955. *(John Oxley)*

North Bridge served both the gas and electric works. Sometimes they couldn't get empty coal wagons out fast enough so incoming traffic had to be stabled in sidings at Brighouse. Holmfield, Pellon and St Pauls received coal. Pellon also had a good trade in timber. Outgoing traffic at Holmfield included biscuits from Meredith & Drew, wool from Smith Bulmer and machinery from Drakes Siding.

The station master's job included canvassing for traffic. Frank would wander up to Drakes and ask the men in the yard 'are you busy lads?' They might reply 'Well we will be when such an' such an order gets moving'. Frank would then go into the office and say that he'd heard that they might have traffic which needed moving to wherever, so could he quote for rail.

St Pauls Station had lost its regular passenger service in 1916 so it was not too surprising that the platform canopy had fallen into disrepair. However inside the booking hall were some unopened crates which had evidently been there for a time. On investigation they contained new panes of glass for the verandah which now stood over the area where they bagged coal. Not wishing to waste BR resources, Frank had the panes sent back.

The route beyond Holmfield to Queensbury was closed in May 1956 and Frank's empire was in decline. When he was promoted to Thornhill, near Dewsbury, in June 1958, the post at Ovenden was abolished, the area then coming under the Halifax Station Master and the Ovenden house going to a permanent way inspector.

Thornhill was on the ex L&Y main line through the Calder Valley between Sowerby Bridge and Wakefield. The post included Dewsbury Market Place. It was altogether a bigger affair than Ovenden but it closed at the end of 1961.

However, Frank had recently been interviewed for the post of senior relief station master. Initially he was based at Wakefield then at Leeds. He continued to live at Thornhill which he found convenient for most of the places he visited even though it no longer had a direct rail service. He could always get a bus to Dewsbury.

His last eight years on the railway saw him again on relief but this time at some of the larger stations including Wakefield Westgate, Leeds Central and Halifax. He says the job was an easy one if nothing went wrong. More often than not it was bad news if somebody came into his office as they usually brought a problem.

At Leeds Central, the duties included looking after VIPs. When the Princess Royal, who lived at Harewood House, travelled to London, she paid with a cheque drawn on Coutts & Co., or at least her lady in waiting did so. One day she turned up with 20 items of luggage which were duly loaded on to the train. Before leaving Frank's office, she asked her lady in waiting 'have you not forgotten something?' – 'I don't think so ma'am' – 'What about the porter's tip?' The lady in waiting produced a shilling. The porter bent double as he crawled out backwards. Then, when he was out of earshot, he muttered 'mean old (person)'.

Frank retired in 1970, a few months short of his 64th birthday. By that time, most of his former Great Northern haunts had disappeared. Many of the stations which remained open had become unstaffed and the institution of station master was about to be abolished.

The verandah at St. Pauls Station could certainly have done with some new panes of glass.
(Martin Bairstow Collection)

Leeds-Doncaster in recent times

Closure of Leeds Central and concentration of business on City Station coincided with an acceleration of the London service.

From 1 May 1967, the 7.30 from Leeds reached Kings Cross non stop at 10.13 finally restoring the schedule achieved by the pre-war streamliners.

This level of performance was achieved only by three Leeds-London trains each way and one Bradford to Kings Cross which ran direct via Wortley West and South Junctions. Apart from these high speed 'Deltic'+ eight coach workings, the rest of the timetable was still pretty leisurely.

The fastest times continued to improve slightly by 1976. But the real change came in 1979 with full implementation of the timetable based on High Speed Trains marketed as 'InterCity 125' with a streamlined class 43 loco at each end. The revolutionary feature here was the consistent speed of trains spaced at regular intervals throughout the day, completing the $185^3/4$ mile journey in under $2^1/2$ hours with as many as six stops.

Electrification was authorised in 1984 and completed in August 1988. The work involved closure of the ex-LNWR viaduct approach to Leeds with all traffic routed via Holbeck. Gelderd Road Junction, created in 1967, was abolished and the track straightened to allow higher speed.

The present London service involves a mixture of electric and diesel trains, operated post privatisation by the Great North Eastern Railway. Since May 1988, there have been 21 departures from Leeds Mondays to Fridays, generally at hourly intervals with extras in the early morning. The fastest time is 1 hour 56 minutes stopping only at Wakefield Westgate but most trains serve Doncaster and up to four other intermediate stations, still reaching the capital in, typically 2 hours 25 minutes.

Local Trains

The local trains between Leeds and Doncaster all but disappeared in November 1967 when stations were closed at Fitzwilliam, Hemsworth and Carcroft & Adwick Le Street. South Elmsall remained open with around six trains each way daily. The practice of serving Wakefield Kirkgate also ceased.

Fitzwilliam reopened in 1982, the first of a number of unstaffed wooden halts financed by the West Yorkshire PTE. Most are on the same sites as former stations but are entirely new structures. Sandal followed in 1987 and Outwood the next year.

In South Yorkshire, where Euro grants are easier to obtain, more substantial structures have appeared at Adwick and at Bentley.

Local trains became hourly in 1987. After the 1988 electrification, they continued to be worked by class 142 and 144 'pacer' diesels until 1989 when life expired class 307 electrics were brought from the London, Tilbury and Southend line. These were replaced in 1990 by three new four car units of class 321.

Since May 1988 there has been a second hourly local between Leeds and Fitzwilliam, a diesel going on to Sheffield. Also, since 1992, there has been an additional hourly diesel between Adwick and Doncaster.

Leeds-Wakefield-Sheffield

Another change in May 1967 was the diversion of most Leeds - Sheffield expresses away from the former Midland Main Line, which missed Wakefield. Instead they followed the same route as the London trains as far as South Kirkby Junction calling at Wakefield Westgate.

In 1973 they were diverted back onto the Midland Main Line because of mining subsidence between South Kirkby and Sheffield. Those which still served Wakefield Westgate were subjected to an arduously slow journey via Kirkgate to reach the Midland Main Line at Oakenshaw South Junction. What was needed was to reinstate the Sandal Curve which had been removed in 1938. Before this was considered seriously, the subsidence problem moved and, from 1984, traffic was again routed via South Kirkby and the Midland Main Line was closed.

142086 calls at the then recently opened Sandal & Agbrigg with a Doncaster to Leeds local on 24 December 1987. *(Martin Bairstow)*

A Class 110 'Calder Valley' set leads a 6 car formation working a local from Leeds Central to Doncaster on 6 July 1965. *(M. Mitchell)*

When coal was still king, 40038 passes a slag heap between Carcroft and Hampole with a northbound mixed freight on 27 December 1973. *(M. Mitchell)*

307122 calls at South Elmsall with a Doncaster to Leeds local on 22 December 1990.
(Martin Bairstow)

A Kings Cross to Leeds electric (Class 91 out of sight in front, driving trailer in rear) passing the new Adwick Station on 2 November 1995.
(Martin Bairstow)

The old building of Carcroft & Adwick-le-Street survives just to the north. 141101, working the Adwick to Doncaster 'Shuttle' is proceeding from its refuge/stabling point on the Carcroft Junction to Skellow Junction curve.
(Martin Bairstow)

The Leeds, Bradford & Halifax Junction today

Bradford Exchange, 10 July 1965. B1 4-6-0 No 61115 prepares to take 'The West Riding' as far as Leeds Central. Alongside are two class 110 'Calder Valley' units. The ten platform terminus closed on 13 January 1973 in favour of a smaller structure 1/4 mile to the south. *(Martin Bairstow Collection)*

Fairburn 2-6-4T No.42152 worked the last steam train out of Bradford Exchange, the 4.18pm to Leeds with through carriages to Kings Cross on Sunday 1 October 1967.

Prior to the closure of Leeds Central, most through carriages from Bradford had been attached to Leeds-Kings Cross trains at Wakefield Westgate. After closure of the Drighlington route, this traffic had gone via the Wortley West to South curve but, from 1 May 1967, all the Bradford portions were joined at Leeds City.

From May 1971 the number of through trains was reduced. Those which continued to run to and from Bradford did so as a full train length of up to ten coaches. When hauled by class 31 locomotives, they could make heavy work of the climb up from Wortley to Armley.

In 1979 the 'Deltics' and class 47s were replaced on Leeds-London by class 43 High Speed Trains. A handful of these continued to and from Bradford Exchange.

There was just one exception to the general rule, an early morning direct Bradford to Kings Cross and early evening return which went direct avoiding Leeds. This ceased first in the northbound direction then in 1984 the southbound departure was diverted via Leeds causing closure of the Wortley West to South curve.

Finally, in 1989 the handful of remaining Bradford through trains were diverted to run from Forster Square leaving Bradford Exchange (Interchange as it had become) without any Inter City trains.

Back in 1967, there were generally two trains an hour between Bradford Exchange and Leeds comprising the loco hauled through carriages to London, the class 110 'Calder Valley' dmus from Manchester and assorted other dmus on Bradford-Leeds locals. In October 1968 cuts were imposed which left some gaps of an hour but these were gradually restored over the next few years. From May 1975, a 20 minute frequency was offered – one of the first fruits of the newly formed West Yorkshire PTE. From 1979, one train per hour started running through to York. In 1987 the basic service was stepped up to quarter hourly and from 1990 every train came through from Halifax or beyond.

Today the hourly pattern gives four trains:

Manchester Victoria- Selby
Blackpool North-York or Scarborough
Manchester Victoria-York
Halifax-Leeds

On Sundays the frequency is at half that level.

The ten platform terminus at Bradford Exchange was replaced on 15 January 1973 by a smaller structure on the south side of Bridge Street. Bramley Station reopened on 12 September 1983 as an unstaffed halt with wooden platforms and five times the train service which it had enjoyed prior to closure 17 years earlier.

Freight traffic slowly dwindled away. Stanningley and Armley Moor closed in 1979 and 1984 respectively. Adolphus Street had closed in1972 as had City Road which took away the triangular junction at St Dunstans.

Steel traffic to Dudley Hill finished in 1981. Latterly this had been worked via Bowling Junction, there being no longer any physical junction at Laisterdyke. In 1985 new pointwork was installed between the remaining sidings at Laisterdyke and the adjacent main line permitting closure of the route to Bowling Junction. At present (1999), the sidings at Laisterdyke are disused though I did see an English, Welsh & Scottish Railway test train there fairly recently.

New Pudsey

Just eight weeks prior to the closure of Leeds Central, on 6 March 1967, an additional station was opened called New Pudsey. Situated 3/4 mile west of Stanningley, it was described as the country's first Inter City park and ride station. It was one of only a tiny handful of stations opened on British Railways during the 1960s.

Contemporary thinking was that the future of passenger rail travel lay only in fast trains to London and precious little else. This begged the question how people were expected to gain access to this future rail network when, even then, road access to city centre stations was becoming increasingly difficult.

The answer was that they could park their cars at a new station situated adjacent to the Leeds Ring Road where they could join through trains to London. At first very few other trains stopped at New Pudsey. The first train in Bradford direction was not until 10.54am, Mondays to Fridays, even later on Saturdays. A few more stops were added from 1 May 1967 and again from September. Only from 1 January 1968 was there a comprehensive local service at New Pudsey following the closure of Stanningley.

There was no Sunday service until June 1981. Previous representations to BR had met with the response 'the station was built for businessmen and businessmen don't travel on Sundays'.

Gradually over the following decades, the original rather special concept of New Pudsey was forgotten. The through London trains were reduced in number then withdrawn altogether. The station assumed a similar function to any other commuter station with a car park. Incoming traffic began to develop with the building of nearby office blocks in the 1980s and the Owlcotes shopping centre in 1990.

155345 coping with 'the wrong kind of snow' at New Pudsey in February 1991.   (Martin Bairstow)

Deltic No D9000 'Royal Scots Grey' approaching the site of New Pudsey Station with Pullman cars for Bradford on 16 October 1965. The area on the right is now the Owlcotes Centre.

(Martin Bairstow Collection)

156475 calls at Bramley bound for York in 1990.   *(Martin Bairstow)*

Appendices

Leeds, Bradford & Halifax Junction

Opened
1\. 8.1854 Leeds Central – Bowling Jn and Bradford Adolphus St
7\. 1.1867 Hammerton St – Mill Lane Jn

Closed to Passengers
6\. 1.1867 Bradford Adolphus St
31.12.1961 Laisterdyke – Bowling Jn
29\. 4.1967 Leeds Central

Closed to all Traffic
29\. 4.1967 Leeds Central
28\. 4.1972 Bradford Adolphus St
Sep 1985 Laisterdyke – Bowling Jn

Miles	Stations	Opened	Closed
0	Leeds Central	18. 9.1848	29. 4.1967
½	Holbeck	2. 7.1855	5. 7.1958
2	Armley Moor	1. 8.1854	2. 7.1966
4	Bramley	1. 8.1854	2. 7.1966
5¼	Stanningley	1. 8.1854	30.12.1967
6	New Pudsey	6. 3.1967	–
7½	Laisterdyke	1. 8.1854	2. 7.1966
	Bradford Adolphus St	1. 8.1854	6. 1.1867
	Bowling	1. 8.1854	31. 1.1895
9	St. Dunstans	21.11.1878	13. 9.1952
9½	Bradford Exchange	9. 5.1850	–

Bramley Station reopened on 12. 9.1983

Doncaster, Wakefield and Leeds

Opened
5\. 10.1857 Ings Road Jn (Wakefield) – Wortley S and W Junctions
1\. 2.1866 Doncaster to Ings Road Jn

Closed
Sep 1984 Wortley South to West

Stations reopened
1\. 3.1982 Fitzwilliam
30.11.1987 Sandal
12\. 7.1988 Outwood
11.10.1993Adwick

Miles	Stations	Opened	Closed
0	Doncaster	7. 9.1848	–
1¾	Bentley	17 5.1993	–
4	Carcroft & Adwick-le-Street	1. 2.1866	4.11.1967
6	Hampole	1. 2.1866	5. 1.1952
8½	South Elmsall	1. 2.1866	–
11¾	Hemsworth	1. 2.1855	4.11.1967
13¼	Fitzwilliam	1. 6.1937	4.11.1967
14¼	Nostell	1. 2.1866	27.10.1951
16	Hare Park & Croft	Nov 1885	2. 2.1952
18	Sandal	1. 2.1866	2.11.1957
19¾	Wakefield Westgate	5.10.1857	–
22¼	Lofthouse & Outwood	1858	11. 6.1960
24¼	Ardsley	5.10.1857	31.10.1964
27¼	Beeston	Feb. 1860	1. 3.1953
29¼	Holbeck	2. 7.1855	5. 7.1958
29¾	Leeds Central	18. 9.1848	29. 4.1967

Ardsley to Laisterdyke

Opened
20\. 8.1856 Gildersome – Laisterdyke
10\. 10.1857 Ardsley – Gildersome

Closed
3\. 7.1966 passengers
28.10.1966 Gildersome – Birkenshaw
13\. 3.1968 Morley Top – Gildersome
13\. 3.1968 Birkenshaw – Dudley Hill
1981 Dudley Hill – Laisterdyke

Miles	Stations	Opened	Closed
0	Ardsley	5.10.1857	31.10.1964
1½	Tingley	May 1859	30. 1.1954
2½	Morley Top	10.10.1857	31.12.1960
4¼	Gildersome	20. 8.1856	11. 6.1955
5½	Drighlington & Adwalton	20. 8.1856	30.12.1961
6½	Birkenshaw & Tong	20. 8.1856	3.10.1953
8¼	Dudley Hill	20. 8.1856	5. 4.1952
10¼	Laisterdyke	1. 8.1854	2. 7.1966

Wakefield Westgate to Drighlington & Adwalton

Opened
Jan. 1862 Wrenthorpe S Junction – Roundwood Colliery (g)
7\. 4.1862 Wakefield Westgate – Flushdyke
19\. 8.1863 Upper Batley – Adwalton Jn
2\. 4.1864 Flushdyke – Ossett
1.11.1864 Batley – Upper Batley
15.12.1864 Ossett – Batley
Jun. 1874 Runtlings Lane Jn – Dewsbury (g)
9\. 9.1874 Ossett – Dewsbury
Mar. 1875 Wrenthorpe N – W Junctions
15\. 3.1880 Dewsbury Jn. – Batley Carr
12\. 4.1880 Batley Car – Batley

Closed to passengers
30\. 6.1909Ossett – Batley
6\. 9.1964 Wakefield W – Adwalton Jn

Closed to all traffic
24\. 3.1956 Runtlings Lane Jn – Shaw Cross
13\. 2.1965 Wrenthorpe S – W Junctions
13\. 2.1965 Roundwood Coll – Adwalton Jn
29.10.1965 Wrenthorpe N Jn – Roundwood Coll
29\. 4.1972 Shaw Cross – Batley

Miles	Stations	Opened	Closed
0	Wakefield Westgate	5.10.1857	–
1¼	Alverthorpe	Oct. 1872	3. 4.1954
3	Flushdyke	7. 4.1862	3. 5.1941
3¾	Ossett	7. 4.1864	5. 9.1964
–	Chickenley Heath	2. 7.1877	30. 6.1909
5¼	Earlsheaton	Jan. 1875	6. 6.1953
	Dewsbury (temp sta)	9. 9.1874	14. 3.1880
6¼	Dewsbury Central	15. 3.1880	5. 9.1964
6¾	Batley Carr	15. 3.1880	4. 3.1950
7¾	Batley	18. 9.1848	–
8½	Upper Batley	19. 8.1863	2. 2.1952
9¼	Howden Clough	1.11.1866	29.11.1952
10¾	Drighlington & Adwalton	20. 8.1856	30.12.1961

(g) = opened to goods traffic only

Halifax High Level

Opened
1\. 8.1890 Holmfield – Pellon (g)
5\. 9.1890 Holmfield – St Pauls

Closed
31.12.1916 Passengers
25\. 6.1960 All Traffic

Miles	Stations	Opened	Closed
0	Holmfield	15.12.1879	21. 5.1955
2¼	Pellon	5. 9.1890	31.12.1916
3	St Pauls	5. 9.1890	31.12.1916

Laisterdyke to Shipley

Opened
Aug. 1874 Goods
15\. 4.1875 Passengers

Closed
31\. 1.1931 Passengers
31.10.1964 Cutlers Jn – Idle
28.10.1966 Laisterdyke – Quarry Gap Jn
5.10.1968 Idle – Shipley

Miles	Stations	Opened	Closed
0	Laisterdyke	1. 8.1854	2. 7.1966
2¾	Eccleshill	15. 4.1875	31. 1.1931
4	Idle	15. 4.1875	31. 1.1931
4½	Thackley	1. 3.1878	31. 1.1931
6¼	Shipley (GN)	15. 4.1875	31. 1.1931

The junction with the Midland at Shipley opened on 1. 11.1875

Bradford Exchange to Halifax and Keighley

Opened
17. 8.1874	Halifax – North Bridge (g)
1. 9.1874	North Bridge – Holmfield (g)
4.12.1876	St Dunstans – Great Horton (g)
4.12.1876	Horton Jn – City Road (g)
9. 7.1877	Great Horton – Clayton (g)
1. 5.1878	Clayton – Thornton (g)
14.10.1878	Bradford Exchange – Thornton
14.10.1878	Queensbury – Holmfield (g)
1.12.1879	Queensbury – Halifax
1. 9.1882	Thornton – Denholme (g)
1. 1.1884	Thornton – Denholme
1. 4.1884	Denholme – Keighley (g)
7. 4.1884	Denholme – Ingrow
1.11.1884	Ingrow – Keighley

Closed to Passengers
21. 5.1955	Bradford – Halifax/Keighley

Closed to all Traffic
26. 5.1956	Queensbury – Holmfield
26. 5.1956	Cullingworth – Ingrow
25. 6.1960	Holmfield – North Bridge
15. 7.1961	Keighley GN Goods
9.11.1963	Thornton – Cullingworth
25. 6.1965	Horton Park – Thornton
25. 6.1965	Ingrow – Keighley
25. 8.1972	St Dunstans – City Road
28. 4.1974	North Bridge – Halifax

	Stations	Opened	Closed
0	Bradford Exchange	9. 5.1850	–
1/2	St Dunstans	21.11.1878	13. 9.1952
1	Manchester Road	14.10.1878	31.12.1915
1¾	Horton Park	1.11.1880	13. 9.1952
2¼	Great Horton	14.10.1878	21. 5.1955
3½	Clayton	14.10.1878	21. 5.1955
4½	Queensbury	12. 7.1879	21. 5.1955
6¾	Holmfield	15.12.1879	21. 5.1955
7¾	Ovenden	2. 6.1881	21. 5.1955
8¾	North Bridge	25. 3.1880	21. 5.1955
9½	Halifax	1. 7.1844	–
6	Thornton	14.10.1878	21. 5.1955
7½	Denholme	1. 1.1884	21. 5.1955
8½	Wilsden	1. 7.1886	21. 5.1955
9¾	Cullingworth	7. 4.1884	21. 5.1955
12½	Ingrow (GN)	7. 4.1884	21. 5.1955
13½	Keighley	16. 3.1847	–

(g) = opened to goods traffic only

Methley Joint

Opened
Jan. 1865	Goods
1. 5.1865	Passengers

Closed
31.10.1964	Passengers
3. 4.1965	West & Newmarket Colliery
25. 3.1967	Methley South – Joint Jn
1980	East of Newmarket Colliery

	Stations	Opened	Closed
0	Ardsley	5.10.1857	31.10.1914
3¾	Stanley	1. 5.1869	31.10.1964
6¼	Methley South	1. 5.1869	5. 3.1960
7¾	Castleford Central	1. 7.1840	–

Pudsey Loop

Opened
1877	Stanningley – Pudsey Greenside (g)
1. 4.1878	Stanningley – Pudsey Greenside
1.11.1893	Bramley – Laisterdyke
1.12.1893	Pudsey Greenside – Low Moor

Closed to Passengers
31. 8.1914	Pudsey Greenside – Low Moor
13. 6.1964	Bramley – Laisterdyke

Closed to all Traffic
30. 9.1917	Dudley Hill – Low Moor
1952	Tyersal Jn – Broad Lane Jn
3. 7.1965	Bramley – Cutlers Jn

	Stations	Opened	Closed
0			
1¼	Bramley	1. 8.1854	2. 7.1966
1¾	Pudsey Lowtown	1. 7.1878	13. 6.1964
3¾	Pudsey Greenside	1. 4.1878	13. 6.1964
4½	Laisterdyke	1. 8.1854	2. 7.1966
6½	Dudley Hill	20. 8.1856	5. 4.1952
	Low Moor	9. 7.1848	12. 6.1965

The Stanningley branch closed when the Bramley line opened.

Batley to Beeston

Opened
Late 1887	Batley – Soothill Colliery
1. 8.1890	Batley – Tingley – Beeston

Closed
27.10.1951	Passengers
4. 7.1953	Batley – Woodkirk
4. 7.1953	Tingley – Beeston
28. 6.1964	Woodkirk – Tingley

	Stations	Opened	Closed
0	Batley	18. 9.1848	–
1¾	Woodkirk	1. 8.1890	23. 9.1939
3	Tingley	May 1859	30. 1.1954
5¾	Beeston	Feb. 1860	1. 3.1953

Conclusion

Recently I heard on television, a quotation made some years ago by a Frenchman predicting that "Railways will be the transport of the twenty first century – if only they can survive the twentieth".

It used to be thought that the growth of road transport would displace the railways. Up to a certain point that is true. But beyond that point, more cars and more lorries actually means a greater need for transport by rail. Not only does the increased road traffic create congestion and pollution, it also affords better access to the rail network. That is why we now see full car parks at New Pudsey, Outwood and Sandal & Agbrigg.

The greater part of the Great Northern mileage in the West Riding did not survive. It is hard to imagine some of the routes having much of a part to play in the modern world: The Halifax High Level, Batley to Beeston, stations such as Queensbury which were just too remote. But what about the Shipley branch which passes through a lot of housing built since the 1931 passenger closure?

Stations at Bramley, Lofthouse & Outwood, Sandal, Fitzwilliam, Carcroft & Adwick le Street were all thought redundant in the 1960s. It was fairly easy to rebuild them when circumstances changed. It is more difficult to do so when the tracks have been removed and the formation sold off for redevelopment.

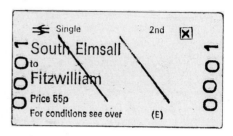

THE END Track is removed from Hewenden Viaduct which had been closed to all traffic in November 1963.
(H. Malham)

NOT THE END 158803 at the east end of Leeds Station in September 1998. Most of the former Leeds, Bradford & Halifax Junction survives as a 'Trans Pennine Express' route.
(Martin Bairstow)